Pre-Evangelization and Young Adult "Native Nones"

Pre-Evangelization and Young Adult "Native Nones"

A New Paradigm for Reaching the Unchurched

Tamra Hull Fromm

PICKWICK *Publications* · Eugene, Oregon

PRE-EVANGELIZATION AND YOUNG ADULT "NATIVE NONES"
A New Paradigm for Reaching the Unchurched

Pickwick Publications
An Imprint of Wipf and Stock Publishers
199 W. 8th Ave., Suite 3
Eugene, OR 97401

www.wipfandstock.com

PAPERBACK ISBN: 978-1-7252-5502-9
HARDCOVER ISBN: 978-1-7252-5503-6
EBOOK ISBN: 978-1-7252-5504-3

Cataloguing-in-Publication data:

Names: Fromm, Tamra Hull, author.

Title: Pre-evangelization and young adult "native nones" : a new paradigm for reaching the unchurched / by Tamra Hull Fromm.

Description: Eugene, OR : Pickwick Publications, 2021 | Includes bibliographical references.

Identifiers: ISBN 978-1-7252-5502-9 (paperback) | ISBN 978-1-7252-5503-6 (hardcover) | ISBN 978-1-7252-5504-3 (ebook)

Subjects: LCSH: Catechetics—Catholic Church. | Catechetics—Catholic Church—History—21st century.

Classification: BX1751.3 .F77 2021 (print) | BX1751.3 .F77 (ebook)

01/18/21

To my husband Brian, in gratitude for his support.

Contents

Tables

Acknowledgments

THIS BOOK, WHICH IS based upon my doctoral dissertation, could not have been written without the guidance and expertise of my supervisors, Dr. Andrew Morris and Dr. Birute Briliute from Maryvale Institute/Liverpool Hope University. They have challenged me to become a better researcher by broadening my perspective on the subject matter.

I would also like to thank Dr. Mary Mills from Maryvale Institute for her encouragement as I churned the dissertation into something readable for a wider audience.

Gratitude is likewise extended to Sr. Arlene Kosmatka, OP, my spiritual director. She enabled me to reflect upon how God has guided me through the research and writing process.

For the priests and RCIA directors in the Archdiocese of Detroit who helped identify catechumens for my qualitative study. And for those young adults who generously shared their faith journeys with me.

To my parents and grandparents, who gave me the gift of a Christian faith and example.

Finally, to my husband Brian for his support and encouragement on so many levels. Throughout this project, you kept me focused, grounded, and moving toward the goal. I thank God every day for you.

And to God, who called, inspired, and sustained me.

Abbreviations

CARA   Center for Applied Research in the Apostolate

CCC   *Catechism of the Catholic Church.* 2nd ed. Washington, DC: United States Catholic Conference, 2000.

CIC   *Code of Canon Law: Latin-English Edition.* Washington, DC: Canon Law Society of America, 1999.

EG   Francis I. *Christus Vivit. Evangelii Gaudium.* Frederick, MD: The Word Among Us, 2013.

EN   Paul VI. *Evangelii Nuntiandi.* Vatican.va.

HCM   Hermeneutical-Communicative Model

IL   Synod of Bishops. *Instrumentum Laboris.* Vatican.va.

NSYR   National Study of Youth and Religion

RM   John Paul II. *Redemptoris Missio.* Vatican.va.

RCIA   Rite of Christian Initiation of Adults

SBNR   Spiritual But Not Religious

USCCB   United States Conference of Catholic Bishops

1

Introduction

IN FEBRUARY 2015, THE Pew Research Center reported in mainstream media from their 2014 Religious Landscape Study that the percentage of Americans ages eighteen and above who self-identified as religiously "unaffiliated" rose from 16.1 to 22.8 percent from 2007 to 2014.[1] This group of so-called "unaffiliated," meaning those individuals who do not identify with any particular religion or faith, are popularly known as the "nones" by American secular and religious media. While numbers in this category increased across all generations, regions, and many demographic groups, including ethnicity, gender, and socio-economic groups, 36 percent were between the ages of 18–24, and 34 percent were between the ages of 25–33;[2] these two age groups are broadly categorized in sociological studies as Millennials or even Generation Z (Gen Z).

Only a few weeks earlier, I had been recently accepted for doctoral studies in theology at Maryvale Institute in Birmingham, England, the home of St. John Henry Newman after his conversion to Catholicism. As part of the application process, I had submitted a preliminary dissertation proposal which would have compared contemporary evangelization methods of Catholics and Protestants with the hope of finding some "common ground."

1. Pew Research Center, "America's Changing Religious Landscape."

2. Pew Research Center, "America's Changing Religious Landscape." These percentages, however, include young adults raised in a religious tradition who now self-identify as "unaffiliated" or "none." Pew claims that approximately 78 percent of formerly Catholic adults left the faith before age 23; Pew Research Center, "Faith in Flux," 21.

Later that month, my husband and I attended an evangelization seminar by Sherry Weddell, cofounder of the Catherine of Siena Institute and author of several books on Catholic discipleship. I approached Weddell during one of the breaks and asked for her insight on where she felt the gaps existed in academic research on evangelization. She explained that the Catholic Church has a rich history and content of catechesis— "we know what to do once we get them in the door"—but what academics need to plumb is the stage of pre-evangelization. The conversation percolated within me for several days.

And then the Holy Spirit kickstarted my curiosity into high gear. I quickly began googling "nones" and reading everything I could find. I scribbled down the questions that were emerging in my mind: Who were these "nones"? And most importantly, how could these "nones" be reached? My dissertation topic shifted almost immediately.

Much Ado about "Nones"

Not surprisingly, one of the most challenging issues facing the post-Vatican II American Catholic Church is the waning religious attendance and practice of young adults.[3] Broadly, statistics from surveys over the past five to ten years have indicated an increase in the percentage of young adults who claim to have no allegiance to or identification with a faith tradition.[4] While some of these same young adults would claim to be "spiritual but not religious,"

3. In this book, I use the term "young adults" as defined by the US bishops in United States Conference of Catholic Bishops, *Sons and Daughters*. They are "persons in their late teens, twenties, and thirties" who represent diverse cultural, racial, ethnic, educational, vocational, social, political, and spiritual backgrounds. They are college and university students, workers, and professionals; they are persons in military service; they are single, married, divorced, or widowed; they are with or without children.

4. Pew Research Center, "US Religious Landscape Survey"; Pew Research Center, "America's Changing Religious Landscape"; Kosmin et al., "American Religious Identification Survey"; Kosmin and Keysar, "American Religious Identification Survey 2008." The findings of all three surveys of the National Study of Youth and Religion, 2002/2003, 2005, and 2007 are chronicled in Smith and Denton, *Soul Searching*; Smith and Snell, *Souls in Transition*; and Smith et al., *Young Catholic America*. The National Study of Youth and Religion, http://youthandreligion.nd.edu/, whose data were used by permission here, was generously funded by Lilly Endowment Inc., under the direction of Christian Smith of the Department of Sociology at the University of Notre Dame, and Lisa Pearce of the Department of Sociology at the University of North Carolina at Chapel Hill.

the increase in the number of "nones" appears to be representative of a continued downward sloping trend of religious attendance.

In response, several books and articles have emerged in American popular and religious media speculating on how this crisis can or should be solved, the trend reversed, and how churches can best reach this demographic.[5] As I am writing this manuscript, the United States Conference of Catholic Bishops (USCCB) devoted a predominant portion of their June 2019 gathering to the discussion of "nones," led by Los Angeles Auxiliary Bishop Robert E. Barron, who is chairman of the bishops' Committee on Evangelization and Catechesis. Clearly it is a hot topic for both Catholics and Protestants.

However, we cannot simply lump all young adult "nones" into one basket. Some young adults tend to loosely believe in a higher power, force, or guidance from the universe. Others may say they believe in God without any attachment to a religious group or faith community. Still others reduce their beliefs to just doing good to others, a lowest common denominator kind of ethicism or moralism. Young adult "nones" may even pick and choose their beliefs from multiple religious traditions, fabricating a kind of "patchwork religion."[6] "Nones" may also include the "dones," or those young adults who have left their childhood or native religion to become unaffiliated.

While much has been written about American young adults leaving parishes and churches, both Catholic and Protestant, less academic work has been done on what attracts the "native nones," or those who were raised without a religious background or affiliation, especially when they are not knocking on our parish doors.

I was interested in these young adult "native nones." Why? In 2015, Pew reported that 67 percent of young adults characterized as Millennials who were raised as "nones" continue to identify as "nones" as adults and are choosing not to join a faith community. In contrast to those Millennials who switch religious faiths or transition to an unaffiliated status, these

---

5. Among the plethora of resources that can be found by simply doing a Google search using the key terms "young adults," "Millennials," and "nones," see White, *Rise of the Nones*; Triska and Triska, "Evangelizing Religious Nones." Many additional articles and books are cited within this book.

6. The term "patchwork religion" comes from Wuthnow, *After the Baby Boomers*, 15. Wuthnow bases his own term on French anthropologist Claude Levi-Strauss' term *bricolage* (French for "tinkering").

"native nones" have among the highest retention rates among Millennials.[7] This means, essentially, that these young adults do not often convert into the Christian faith—or any faith, for that matter. So I was interested in what actually did attract or prompt young adult "native nones" to make an initial decision to investigate the Catholic faith.[8]

What This Book Is About

This book explores the early conversion experiences of twenty-four American young adults who did not practice a Christian faith tradition in their childhood or adolescence and the role of pre-evangelization in the conversion process. I do not intend to address the phenomenon of the many young adults in the United States who have left the Catholic Church (or any other Christian denomination) after having been baptized or confirmed. While relevant, I will not attempt to answer all the "whys" which may keep young adults away from participating in traditionally associated Christian religious practices, such as attending Mass or other liturgies. I believe that the principles and characteristics of the New Evangelization are most applicable to this audience.[9] Rather, my interest and the focus

---

7. Pew Research Center, "America's Changing Religious Landscape." Further, in contrast to a possible claim that young adult "nones" may switch to a faith tradition as they grow older, Pew suggests that generational cohorts become less religiously affiliated as they age.

8. Throughout this book I have cited research by Van Dop, "Connecting to God," and Vielma, "Catholic Conversion Process." Van Dop's dissertation examines the factors that have affected a small group of converts (sample size of 56) in the Vineyard Church in Columbus, Ohio. Vielma's thesis focuses on a very small sample (i.e., six participants) of university students in the southwest region of the United States who choose to convert to Catholicism, however only one of the participated was described as "unaffiliated" in terms of faith; the remaining participants were converts from a Protestant denomination (i.e., Baptist or Church of Christ).

9. The term "New Evangelization," coined by Pope John Paul II in Haiti in 1983, is later defined in *Redemptoris Missio* as applicable "particularly in countries with ancient Christian roots . . . where entire groups of the baptized have lost a living sense of the faith, or even no longer consider themselves members of the Church, and live a life far removed from Christ and his Gospel . . . [W]hat is needed is a 'new evangelization' or a 're-evangelization.'" This definition might suggest that the primary purpose of the New Evangelization is to draw back those baptized or otherwise sacramentalized (i.e., those who have received the sacraments of Baptism, Eucharist, or even Confirmation) Catholic young adults who have left the active practice of the Catholic faith.

of this research is on the "native nones," or those young adults who were raised unaffiliated, "unchurched," or nonreligious.

I argue that these young adult "native nones" may require a different approach in evangelization. Instead of boldly proclaiming the Gospel of Jesus Christ (defined as the "*kerygma*") at the outset, a more rudimentary or elementary preparation—a pre-evangelization—may be needed so that the Gospel may be more clearly understood.[10] Pre-evangelization, according to Fr. Alfonso Nebreda's original definition of the term back in the 1960s, is a "stage of preparation for the *kerygma* which, taking the [human person] as he is and where he is, makes a human dialogue possible and awakens in him the sense of God, an indispensable element for opening his heart to the message."[11]

Nearly forty years ago, the American Catholic Church acknowledged "a great need in the United States . . . to prepare the ground for the gospel message."[12] The National Catechetical Directory for the United States cites several cultural reasons for the need of this preparation: a lack of religious affiliation, a radical questioning of values, pluralism, and increased population mobility."[13] In chapter 2, I propose some additional cultural factors. In contrast to relying upon a formal catechesis or teaching which begins at the parish, I propose that pre-evangelization begins at the secular level and may hold the key toward stimulating unchurched young adults in the United States to become more open to the Gospel of Jesus Christ.

Because much of the focus of the American Catholic Church over the past ten to fifteen years has been on the New Evangelization and the preaching of the *kerygma*, I suggest that reaching this audience requires a shift toward a new paradigm. When I use the term "paradigm" in this context, I mean a set of beliefs or values, shared by members of the American Catholic Church, that guide our actions. Our beliefs and values are informed by how we perceive reality, how we absorb knowledge, and how we have responded to these. A paradigm shift therefore implies that there has been a fundamental change in the approach or underlying assumptions of what we have and what we now believe and hence, what we do now.[14]

10. John Paul II differentiates the *kerygma* from catechesis in *Catechesi Tradendae*, 25.

11. Nebreda, *Kerygma*, viii.

12. USCCB, *Sharing the Light*, 34.

13. USCCB, *Sharing the Light*, 34.

14. Thomas Kuhn states that paradigms are "universally recognized scientific

What do I mean by this? First of all, I submit that American Christians may be taking for granted the foundations which previously enabled the gospel message to take root. Because the religious landscape has changed, Christians (and in particular, Catholics) may need to rethink the way evangelization is done. For example, do clergy and pastoral workers still implicitly assume or presume that "native nones" understand terms such as "sin" or "salvation"? Are they still operating under a belief that if we just keep pushing the truth on them, the "nones" will get it?

Evangelical Tim Buechsel claims that one of the primary reasons why churches fail to effectively evangelize is because they have not adjusted their approach to a post-Christendom world.[15] He adds that many American churches have often fallen prey to the tenets of McDonaldization, which include efficiency, calculability, predictability, and control; in other words, he implies that Christians are accustomed to (and, I would add, prefer) a "one method suits all."[16] Alan Hirsch likewise claims that "ninety-five percent of American churches are using a model that, even if successful, will reach less than half the population."[17] In other words, parishes and churches continue to employ the same language, message, and forms of outreach and expect the same results of their efforts. I agree that these criticisms are equally applicable to Catholics who continue to cling to a pre-Vatican II understanding that we can keep young adults in the Church simply through birth or heritage, rather than reaching outside of the boundaries of the parish campus to engage them.

Both Catholic and Protestant theologians who have studied and ministered to American young adults seem to connect the growing cultural differences between the ecclesial and secular to the situation that Christian missionaries overseas faced in the early twentieth century. Catholic documents from Vatican II speak of the mission *ad gentes*, or a kind of evangelization that is directed toward persons in non-Christian countries who have never heard the gospel message.[18] Hostetler and Anderson

achievements that for a time provide model problems and solutions to a community of practitioners." Kuhn, *Structure of Scientific Revolutions*, viii. He later claims that a paradigm change (or shift) occurs because of discovered anomalies based on observations that result in a crisis out of a conviction that the existing paradigm fails to fit reality.

15. See ch. 5, 167–85, in Buechsel, "One Size Fits All?"

16. Buechsel, "One Size Fits All?," 155–61.

17. Hirsch, *Forgotten Ways*, 36. Hirsch speaks of a "contemporary church growth" model that is attractive to professional, middle-class families in the United States.

18. Rymarz, "Principles of the New Evangelization," 145.

claim that, instead of a familiar territory in which Christianity is widely embraced, we are quickly becoming a foreign land which is resistant to accustomed ways of evangelization.[19] Dan Kimball, a Protestant youth and young adult minister, likens the evangelization of unchurched young adults to mission territory.[20]

Thus, I suggest that by revisiting the circumstances, rationale, and approaches utilized in evangelization to traditional non-Christian cultures and countries, we may discover some keys to unlocking the "enigma of the *kerygma*" for American young adults.

My Own Religious Journey

In some ways, the topic and focus for my dissertation and this book evolved over the past nineteen years since my own conversion to Roman Catholicism. I grew up in a small rural village near the Michigan-Ohio border in a conservative German Lutheran family. I regularly attended Sunday school in the Evangelical Lutheran Church of America (ELCA) and experienced a thorough religious catechesis in this faith as a child and adolescent. However, I questioned what I perceived as a heavy emphasis on morality and rules and fell away from the practice of my faith in my undergraduate years at Michigan State University. I experienced a powerful "born-again" experience during the summer before my senior year and joined a nondenominational quasi-Pentecostalist student faith community, which regularly practiced the use of charismatic gifts (such as speaking in tongues and healing). During my twenties and early thirties, I attended Baptist churches, whose beliefs tended to be Reformed or Calvinistic, but did not necessarily embrace the charismatic dimension of Pentecostalism.

At age thirty-three, I was considering getting married to my at-the-time boyfriend, who was coming back or "reverting" to his native Catholic faith. I agreed to attend the Rite of Christian Initiation for Adults (RCIA) to check out "this Catholic thing . . . but no promises." At the Easter Vigil, I was confirmed into the Catholic Church. My own conversion resulted from influences of Catholic radio and reading the works of the saints, particularly Augustine, Teresa of Avila, and John of the Cross. While I was not a "none," I am personally familiar with the RCIA process.

---

19. Hostetler, "Who Changed the Cultural Channel?," 43; Anderson, *Church for the Twenty-First Century*, 17.

20. Kimball, *They Like Jesus*.

Soon after my conversion, I began working in a local parish as a lay minister to Catholic young adults. During this time, I had the opportunity to discuss faith and spirituality with many young adults. I quickly discovered that many of them were unfamiliar with what I considered basic tenets of Christianity, not to mention Catholicism.

I have since worked in the diocesan Catholic school department in marketing and for the diocesan seminary in admissions, as well as teaching various undergraduate level courses in theology and scripture to laypersons (including those discerning lay pastoral positions, as well as the permanent diaconate and priesthood). I also teach selected topics for the RCIA program at my local parish. I consider myself faithful to the Magisterial teaching of the Catholic Church, yet sensitive to the knowledge and experience which can be drawn from our Protestant brothers and sisters.

During this same time, I was pursuing a graduate degree in theology with a concentration in the New Evangelization. In one of my courses, I wrote a research paper on Adoniram Judson, a Baptist missionary to Burma (now Myanmar) in the 1800s; I was intrigued by his method of first interacting and forming relationships with the Burmese people before explicitly preaching the gospel. I began to wonder what the various Christian confessional bodies could learn from each other in terms of evangelization.

Thus, my own religious journey exposed me academically and experientially to the primary theological differences between Catholics and many Protestant denominations. I also witnessed how evangelization was conducted (or not conducted) by these religious groups.

Outline of the Book

The overarching question that this book seeks to answer is: "How do we prepare unchurched American young adults to hear and accept the Gospel of Jesus Christ?" Supporting this question are the sub-questions, basically: "How did we get here?"; "What is pre-evangelization?"; "What does pre-evangelization look like in practice?"; "What are young adults saying about their early conversion experiences?"; and "Where do we go now?" The outline of the book will align with these questions.

The first section of this book will review the contemporary cultural context of American young adults as the foundation in which "native nones" have grown up. In chapter 2, I argue that selected characteristics of the American culture, including the demise of the metanarrative, the rise of pluralism, individualism, materialism, religious illiteracy, and changes in lifestyle patterns have negatively contributed to "nones" predisposition to and reception of the gospel message.

The second section focuses on pre-evangelization in terms of theory, current practice, and proposed application. Despite the greater emphasis on the New Evangelization in the past several years, I would estimate that many American Catholics, both clergy and laity, have never heard of pre-evangelization, even though the term has been used in Catholic catechetical circles for over sixty years. Within official (or magisterial) Catholic teaching since the Second Vatican Council, the term "evangelization" has been broadly inclusive of many activities, however it is generally understood within the overall mission of the Church to include three stages: pre-evangelization, evangelization, and catechesis.

Chapters 3–6 provide an overview of pre-evangelization from its origins at the Bangkok Catechetical Study Week in 1962. Chapter 4 examines the concept of pre-evangelization through the writings of Fr. Alfonso Nebreda and magisterial documents. In chapter 5, I propose that the locus of the initial significant encounter for "native nones" has moved outside the church (*ad extra*). While I am primarily exploring pre-evangelization from a Roman Catholic perspective, chapter 6 will include insights and examples from Protestant faith traditions and methods with the intent to discover possible synergies and pastoral applications.

The third section examines the current praxis of pre-evangelization. Chapter 7 proposes the Hermeneutical-Communicative Model (HCM) as a lens through which pre-evangelization can be viewed as a first stage in the conversion process. Chapter 8 looks at six examples of pre-evangelization from Catholic and Protestant ministries (i.e., L'Abri, Taizé, Alpha, Nightfever, "conversational evangelism," and digital pre-evangelization) to illustrate what pre-evangelization may look like in both the parish and secular settings. Each method is briefly evaluated according to the findings of my research.

Chapter 9 will look at the early conversion experiences of twenty-four unbaptized young adults (ages 20–35) in the Archdiocese of Detroit who sought information on the Catholic faith through the Rite of Christian Initiation for Adults (RCIA) since 2015. The RCIA is the normative (or usual) process through which adults become catechized and baptized into the Roman Catholic Church. Thus, by choosing to participate in the RCIA, an individual demonstrates that he or she is personally and actively seeking further information on what the Catholic Church teaches. The chapter reveals, through their own voices, common experiences by young adult "native nones" leading up to their participation in the RCIA.

What emerges from this study is, first, the realization that these "native nones" are only one or two generations away from practicing Catholics. Parents are clearly not passing down the faith, which will likely result in continued growing numbers of "native nones." Second, the pivotal encounter takes place in a secular environment, not in the parish or church; this means that laity will need to become more familiar and comfortable with pre-evangelization. Third, pre-evangelization is decidedly more relationally rather than cognitively based; this means that young adult "nones" need to feel connected to someone they trust, someone who answers their questions, and someone who does not judge them before they take the step of plunging into a seeking mode. They do not need a heavy-handed explanation of the *kerygma* or an apologetics to convince them why they should convert.

How do parishes and churches respond to this paradigm shift? In chapter 10, I conclude with implications for parishes, clergy, and laity. I offer practical suggestions for those who seek to attract and evangelize young adult "native nones" within the parish and secular community. Because the need to evangelize young adults crosses denominational boundaries, I will also briefly address some future directions for dialogue how Catholics and Protestants might better collaborate in ministry toward the common goal of fulfilling the church's mission.

Who Is This Book For?

This book is written primarily for clerical and lay audiences of those engaged in pastoral practice as well as an academic audience with interests in the areas of culture and *ethos* of young adults of the current generation. Because of the limited study on pre-evangelization in general, I suggest this book offers a starting point for discussion and evaluation among clergy and laity. Broadly, it may also interest anyone of Christian faith who has likewise observed the trends described in this chapter and then lamented what can be done in response.

If you are looking for a quick fix or a "one size fits all" solution from this book, I will honestly admit that I do not believe there is a simplistic model or method of pre-evangelization. Conversion cannot be manipulated by a formula. Rather, in all its various stages, conversion is a mystery of the interaction between the revelation of God and the free response of the human person. Christians are called to cooperate with God, responding to the call of Christ in Matthew 28:19 to "make disciples of all nations," while at the same time fully respecting the free will of the human agent.

At the same time, I believe the insights from this micro-study of "nones" and a comparative look at pre-evangelization will provide a fresh perspective on how to better address this growing group of individuals in our society. For clergy and pastoral workers, this means becoming more aware of those who do not speak the same religious language or have the same cultural backdrop of the faith. When "nones" do show up at the parish, it means creating a welcoming environment and opportunities for encountering transcendence. It means being willing to be patient with their unique journey and answer their questions. For laypersons, this means you do not need to be a theologian or apologist. Just by living a life of holiness, being willing to approach others, and answering questions without putting on the hard sell can attract and spur on the kind of curiosity which can launch the adventure/pursuit of faith.

So, before we get to the actual research, I think it is critical to recognize that young adults face different challenges with regards to Christianity than previous generations. Some of these can be real obstacles or stumbling blocks to the proclamation of the gospel. In the next chapter, I will unpack the contemporary cultural context which may influence American young adults as they make choices about faith and spirituality.

2

Cultural Context of American Young Adults

> It is obvious . . . that we should take into account the influence of
> the environment on the individual . . . [one] has not only to work
> on the individual but on the structure and on the mentality of the
> milieu which influence him.[1]

IT IS PROBABLY NO surprise that contemporary American young adults live
in a distinct cultural context compared to that of their parents and grandparents. Traditionally, American young adults might have been expected
to follow in the religious footsteps of their parents and grandparents. They
would have attended a church, parish, or synagogue out of a tribal loyalism
or default faith. But today, the situation is different.

In this chapter, I will explore this context in order to demonstrate how
certain elements of the culture may affect young adults' predisposition to
be open to hear and to respond to the *kerygma*. I suggest that a combination of values associated with postmodernity and American culture have
negatively influenced contemporary young adults toward their reception
of the gospel message. Yet young adulthood is also a period of frequent
change, which includes aspects of faith. The ubiquitous influence of technology upon young adults introduces a mixture of positive and negative
effects on how information and communication is received and shaped.
Despite these challenges, I maintain that a new approach and paradigm for
reaching young adults may offer hope.

---

1. Nebreda, "East Asian Study Week," 724.

Changes in Young Adults and Religion

I think it is critical to remember that this situation did not happen overnight. Studies on the relationship between religion and American young adults growing up after the Second Vatican Council have burgeoned in response to their absence from the church pews. Some of the earliest research was conducted by Dean Hoge, Tom Beaudoin, Robert Bellah, and Jeffrey Arnett.[2] Beaudoin's study debunked the myth that young adults tend to return to the church after marriage and/or the birth of children. Instead, young adults have reacted to the church with either skepticism or even indifference. Bellah coined the term "Sheila-ism" after a young adult female named Sheila, in reference to how young adults tend to pick and choose what they want to believe, thus crafting together an individualistic faith. These studies, while they provide excellent insight, primarily addressed young adults typed as Gen X.

More recent research on the religious beliefs of American young adults has been conducted by American sociologists and psychologists such as Christian Smith, Robert Wuthnow, Linda Mercadante, Jean Twenge, and Thomas Rausch. American sociologist Rodney Stark and Canadian philosopher Charles Taylor have provided additional cultural perspectives of the environment in which young adults have grown up and the factors which have influenced their attitudes and beliefs toward religion.

In terms of statistical data on young adults and religion, I am grateful to the Pew Research Center, the Center for Applied Research in the Apostolate (CARA), the American Religious Identification Survey, Barna Group, and the National Study of Youth and Religion (NSYR).[3] These organiza-

2. Hoge et al., *Young Adult Catholics*; Beaudoin, *Virtual Faith*; Bellah, *Habits of the Heart*; Arnett, *Emerging Adulthood*.

3. The Pew Research Center is an independent American think tank based in Washington, DC, which tracks not only American religious beliefs but also, for example, beliefs on politics and policy; use of internet, science, and technology; and social and demographic trends. Because Pew is nonpartisan as well as nonprofit, its polling results theoretically can be unbiased and reliable; the Center for Applied Research in the Apostolate (CARA) is an American nonprofit research affiliated with Georgetown University that conducts social scientific studies on the Catholic Church. Its primary purpose is to serve Catholic dioceses, parishes, academic institutions, media, and members in general with research on religious practices and beliefs. CARA operates a blog entitled Nineteen Sixty-Four (1964), maintained by Mark Gray, which comments on its research studies; the American Religious Identification Survey (ARIS), renamed from the National Survey of Religious Identification, was conducted in both 2001 and 2008 by Barry Kosmin and Ariela Keysar of Trinity College in Hartford, Connecticut. Kosmin, who self-identifies

tions have tracked new developments and trends among young adults and their religious practices (or lack thereof).

Out of various sociological and pastoral writings, I suggest three aspects of the contemporary culture which, when combined, may arguably affect the need for pre-evangelization of American young adults. These are: (1) the philosophical movement associated with postmodernity, (2) American culture, and (3) the unique challenges of the period of young adulthood. I am not going to provide a complete overview of these three aspects; however, I will touch upon those which may most affect young adults' perception of religious beliefs and, notably, their openness to the *kerygma*.

Postmodernity

Almost every book or article that I read while doing my research consistently (and often negatively) referenced the values and *ethos* of postmodernity in which contemporary American young adults have grown up. While I do not intend to unpack the complexity of the terms "postmodernity" or "postmodernism," I want to briefly propose several elements which may serve as a framework of contrast for religion and religious practice.

For example, the premodern period in Western culture could be roughly defined as covering the years AD 30 through 1500. This period was characterized by common values and roots. Divine revelation and recognized authorities (e.g., Catholic Church) determined what was considered

as a "none," and his colleagues attempted to show that "nones" could not universally be identified as atheists but rather considered "spiritual" and "rational skeptics"; Barna Group is a Christian research organization, founded by George Barna and now run by David Kinnaman. While Barna Group is primarily associated with Evangelical Christianity, it also conducts polling and research for other Christian denominations and nonprofit organizations; the NSYR was perhaps the most extensive longitudinal study on American young adults, which explored changes in spirituality and religiosity and provided a rich source of data on the spiritual lives of adolescents as they transitioned into young adults. The NSYR was sponsored by two large nonprofit grants and directed by sociologist Christian Smith of the University of Notre Dame. Smith and his coauthors gathered three waves of data between 2003 and 2008 on American adolescents between the ages 13–17, tracking their religious beliefs and practices as they grew into young adults. Initially, 3,290 adolescents were surveyed by phone, followed by personal interviews with 267 in 45 American states. In 2005, a second telephone survey was conducted with these same subjects, with 122 reinterviewed. In 2007–2008, 2,458 were surveyed again, followed by 230 personal interviews. Smith's series of studies and findings are extensively cited in writings on young adults. However, the NSYR stopped following the targeted group of young adults at the ages of 18–23 years.

true and knowledge was transmitted through a central belief system. Spirituality was marked by transcendence and communication conducted largely by writing; however, written materials were not widely available to all persons.[4] People lived in an "enchanted world," where external and impersonal forces impacted lives as if through a porous veil.[5] While these factors do not indicate that everyone shared the same faith or practice, I suggest they imply a more readily accepted body of beliefs based upon dependence on an external agency or institution.

When we look at the modern period, roughly spanning 1500 through 1950, the locus of knowledge and truth turned away from an external authority and revelation toward human reasoning; therefore, any proposed truth had to be verified by rational or empirical findings.[6] Spirituality shifted towards an individual interiority, while communication shifted to mass printing.[7] Taylor posits that science created a buffered veil between persons, which unlinked the connection with the external world and prompted a disengaged, detached individualism.[8] These elements suggest an epistemological shift from the external to the internal, which resulted in a bridled skepticism of religious tenets with ultimate truth dependent upon scientific evidence.

The postmodern period, which emerged in intellectual circles around 1950 and arguably continues until the present, represents yet another shift against the emphasis on empirical data. In contrast to the solidity of external authority and science, the deconstruction and diffusion of truth has led to an "age of uncertainty."[9] Spirituality is now characterized by creativity, while communication is conducted through electronics.[10]

---

4. Griffin et al., *Varieties of Postmodern Theology*, 108.

5. Taylor, *Secular Age*, 32, 38.

6. Hoffman and Kurzenberger, "Premodern, Modern, and Postmodern," 68–69.

7. Griffin et al., *Varieties of Postmodern Theology*, 108.

8. Taylor, *Secular Age*, 38.

9. According to Hoffman and Kurzenberger, "Premodern, Modern, and Postmodern," 69–70, while ultimate truth cannot be known, localized "truth" or interpretations of central tenets can be accepted and may be even more important.

10. Griffin et al., *Varieties of Postmodern Theology*, 108. Interestingly, the authors make this claim in 1989 when the World Wide Web, now commonly referred to as the internet, was arguably in its infancy stage. Since their writing, communication through electronics has burgeoned through media such as email, social media, and various mobile devices such as smartphones.

Synthesizing these elements, I propose four associated characteristics of the contemporary culture: (1) the lack of objective truth, (2) the demise of the metanarrative, (3) relativism, and (4) individualism. While each of these characteristics could be viewed in isolation, they are also strongly connected, intertwined, and perhaps even dependent upon each other; likewise, they may also impact both how knowledge is received (epistemology) and how events or phenomena are perceived (phenomenology).

Lack of Objective Truth

Postmodernity is sometimes identified with belief in a lack of objective truth. Here again, I do not intend to analyze how this belief began to permeate our culture. However, from a philosophical viewpoint, we might consider the influences of Jacques Derrida and Michel Foucault. Derrida's iconic phrase "nothing outside of the text" can be interpreted to mean that nothing can be understood outside of its context.[11] This may imply that no external or transcendent reality may read or interpret truth or meaning into a specific word or phrase. Rather, truth is known through experience and perceived subjectively, while reality is both imagined and created by the individual. Foucault suggested the impossibility of reaching truth when what we study and how we study the subject is constructed and conditioned (or even represented) as a historical product of power.[12] So-called "truths" are the products of a language which is produced by those in power structures and not by an independent objective reality. In other words, power determines truth.

If we apply this hermeneutic, the Catholic Church might be considered the dominant power in the premodern period. The Church, therefore, determined truth and exercised the means to defend and proclaim. However, in the modern period, science and reason become the centers of power. Finally, in the post-modern society, the individual can be viewed as a power unto oneself, capable of knowing truth through one's own experience. Truth is perceived subjectively, while reality is both imagined and created by the individual. I also suggest that, due to the pervasive influence of social media, there is a growing democratization of truth, meaning that each person has a vote on what defines truth and yet the final decision is made by the majority.

11. Literally, "*il n'y a pas d'hors-texte.*" Derrida, *Of Grammatology,* 158.

12. Foucault, *Power/Knowledge,* 131–33.

Growing up under this worldview, young adults may have difficulty acknowledging an objective, shared reality beyond the self and, even further, that an objective reality could serve as a reliable reference point and impact their lives in some way. This does not mean that young adults are immoral or even amoral. Smith found that young adults articulate a vague sense of morality, expressed by a core principle not to hurt others, and many also indicated a kind of karmic belief in which one's good or bad actions will seemingly return to reward or punish them. Yet they were not sure where or how they understood this.[13]

Instead, young adults base right and wrong upon "common sense," subjective feeling, and being in tune with one's sovereign self.[14] As an example, both Smith and Wuthnow noted that, when questioned about their beliefs, young adults tended to begin their responses with the subjective reference, "I think" or "I believe that" as opposed to referencing what their parents, culture, or religious community taught.[15] Young adults themselves become "social constructionists" who "mostly unquestioningly presuppose that most things . . . are not fixed or given facts of nature but rather [are] human constructions invented through shared social definitions" which can be changed.[16]

If young adults do not view truth or the origin of truth as an external concept or something outside of themselves, then the individual's perception of truth may become internalized. The existence and identity of God likewise may become reduced or reconstructed into whatever the individual wishes God or "god" to be. Smith notes that a common religious theme among teens and young adults is Moralistic Therapeutic Deism (MTD), a nebulous set of beliefs where God becomes somewhat of a remote, divine genie who helps but does not demand anything from humans but a reasonably ethical lifestyle that does not hurt another.[17]

Further, without an objective truth, appealing to God as a transcendent higher power may be nearly impossible with young adults. One cannot claim

13. Smith and Snell, *Souls in Transition*, 45, 47.

14. Smith and Snell, *Souls in Transition*, 46, 49. Pew's 2014 Religious Landscape Study of both "younger" and "older" Millennials indicates 75–79 percent of respondents say that right or wrong "depends on the situation" vs. clear standards for right and wrong. Forty-nine percent said that "common sense" was their source of guidance for right and wrong vs. religion.

15. Wuthnow, *God Problem*, 179; Smith and Snell, *Souls in Transition*, 49.

16. Smith and Snell, *Souls in Transition*, 50.

17. Smith and Snell, *Souls in Transition*, 154–56.

that there is a universal truth applicable to all human beings. This makes the *kerygma* (or the gospel message of Jesus Christ) only one among many narratives, or perhaps even viewed as a myth. Therefore, we cannot begin a conversation based upon a perceived common ground.

Because of this, the approach may need to become more dialogical. The role of the believer is not to make assumptions or judgements about the other. Rather, the exchange becomes an attempt to unpack the layers of unbelief and rationale for any misunderstandings. Such a new paradigm, I suggest, implies a longer conversion period.

Farewell to the Metanarrative

With the demise of the acceptance of objective truth, young adults have become skeptical about metanarratives. A metanarrative may be defined as an overarching story which claims to explain various events and gives meaning by appealing to universal reason or structure.[18] Christianity may be considered an example of such a metanarrative. If young adults share this same outlook, then a kerygmatic message, which is initially proposed as a universal truth, may be immediately rejected.

Yet, Ford believes that conversion takes place through a collision of narratives which can be present in an evangelistic context; he argues that individuals connect more at the point of personal experiences and the expressed experience with God or the divine.[19] Hence, pre-evangelization may be more effective by first appealing to the micro or local narrative; in other words, a story.[20] Stories, as opposed to theological and doctrinal facts, may be more effective in reaching someone who is unfamiliar with theological language typically associated with the proclamation of the *kerygma*.[21] Further, stories of faith shared by a respected witness, whether this is a family member, friend, or coworker, may contain a greater weight of authenticity.

18. Smith and Snell, *Souls in Transition*, 101; Phan, "Evangelization"; Lyotard, *Postmodern Condition*, xxiv.

19. Ford, *Power of Story*, 14.

20. Van Dop, "Connecting to God," 86. Further, Rambo notes the difference between a macro (cultural), micro (family, neighborhood, religious community), and individual (experiences and decision points of the person him or herself) context, which I argue may affect both the nature and reception of the narrative. See Rambo, *Understanding Religious Conversion*, 20–23.

21. McKinney, "Using Storytelling."

"It's All Relative"

When previously held metanarratives are deprived of their authority, Adams suggests a plurality of values will fill the lacuna, without any singular value system being universally legitimized and accepted.[22] Smith and Kinnaman found that many young adults believe that all religions share the same basic principles.[23] This outlook is associated with relativism, which basically means that "every belief on a certain topic, or perhaps about any topic, is as good as every other."[24] Contemporary young adults seem to embrace this diversity.[25] If all religions or lack of religious beliefs are perceived by young adults as relative, I suspect that a method of evangelization characterized by public proclamation of the *kerygma* may be initially viewed as lack of tolerance of another's choice of belief system or even a form of proselytism.

Centrality of the Individual

Contemporary young adults are often described as having grown up in a hyper-individualistic culture, which places an excessive focus on the individual and his or her desires. Religion for young adults is considered a private, individual matter.[26] Moreover, Twenge's research on the relationship between the indicators of individualism and religious practice and doctrine among contemporary teens (who will eventually become young adults) showed an indirect correlation; if she is correct, when individualism rises, religion declines.[27]

However, a decline in the practice of religion may be less due to the explicit rejection of God or Jesus or the church itself and more because of a shift in the way in which young adults choose to practice religion or not at all. Rather than believing or attending religious services out of obligation, British sociologist Grace Davie claims that a culture of consumption promotes a kind of spirituality or religion that can be adopted when young adults want it and when it makes sense to them; Dulles agrees

22. Adams, "Toward a Theological Understanding."

23. Smith and Snell, *Souls in Transition*, 145–46; Kinnaman and Lyons, *unChristian*, 25.

24. Rorty, *Consequences of Pragmatism*, 166.

25. *IL*, 8–9.

26. Kinnaman and Lyons, *unChristian*; Smith and Snell, *Souls in Transition*; Twenge, *iGen*.

27. Twenge, *iGen*, 138.

that the American consumerist culture facilitates a kind of market-driven individualism with regards to religion.[28] Religion or spirituality becomes not only the individual's choice, but its tenets must also resonate with the individual and make sense in terms of the individual where they are and as they understand themselves to be.[29]

An individualistic spirituality does not mean one's set of beliefs is completely or even whimsically fabricated out of nothing. So-called "spiritual but not religious" young adults may choose not to associate with or join traditional religious groups out of a sense of integrity with their own set of beliefs when these are felt to be in incongruence with the religious group's norms.[30] Thus, I suggest that a healthy skepticism about adopting a particular religious belief may both extend the time needed for possible conversion, but more importantly increase the likelihood that a decision is consciously and freely made.

Such a self-referential, individualistic spirituality has given rise to a variety of terms. Coined by Kinnaman, "mono-spirituality" reflects the type of belief or *ethos* which centers around the individual self.[31] Wuthnow believes that young adults craft together a "patchwork religion" by selectively embracing and denying doctrines and beliefs that meet their own understanding and piece these together, like a patchwork quilt, in a way that makes sense to them. The propensity towards "patching" increases with the acceptance of pluralism, expansion of available information, and exposure to diverse cultures and networks.[32] The term "cafeteria believer" is an analogy to dining in a cafeteria where an individual may choose a particular religious tenet or spiritual practice that is desired, but ignore the remainder of the set of practices or beliefs of that same body of faith.[33] I like to use the term "cut-and-paste" spirituality, which refers to the action of electronically deleting text or graphics from one location in a virtual document and adding it to another.

---

28. Davie, "Is Europe an Exceptional Case?," 23–34: 27; Dulles, "Impact of the Catholic Church," 20.

29. Taylor, *Secular Age*, 486, 507.

30. Mercadante, "Seeker Next Door," 31.

31. Barna Group, "David Kinnaman and Jon Tyson Discuss Millennials."

32. Wuthnow, *After the Baby Boomers*, 15. Wuthnow bases his own term on French anthropologist Claude Levi-Strauss' term *bricolage* (French for "tinkering").

33. Smith and Snell, *Souls in Transition*, 167.

If young adults are largely influenced and motivated by individualism, Reed suggests that any evangelistic approach which wishes to reach this demographic at the level of their values must take the form of either enhancing utilitarian or expressive individualism.[34] By this, he means that the approach needs to include a rationale for why the belief makes sense for the individual or how it will enhance the individual's well-being. While I agree in theory with Reed's proposition that believers in dialogue with young adults may speak of the experiential benefits of Christianity to the individual, I disagree that the central message of Christianity should be diminished to appeal exclusively to the subject, which is incompatible with the gospel's countercultural and antithetical theme of denying the self.[35]

Curiously, an excessively individualistic culture may have mixed effects on young adults in terms of affiliation and attachment to a religious community. Wuthnow suggests that contemporary society is defined by loose connections and porous institutions.[36] In other words, young adults are less likely to become attached to groups and organizations. They may visit parishes and even volunteer for a faith-based project, but they do not readily invest themselves by becoming formal members through registration or another rite of belonging. Similarly, groups and institutions may become unable to retain members.

Fr. Michael Gallagher proposes that a frenetic and individualistic lifestyle accompanied by superficial relationships in contemporary Western culture has led to a "wounding" in the sense of belonging. This "wounding" results in a sense of restlessness and yet, at the same time, leaves one without an ability to commit to a group.[37] Based upon research data on why young adults tend to avoid institutional religious communities and my own ministerial experience, I agree with this assessment. Social media has often served to isolate young adults from each other, which impacts their ability to develop and understand social norms leading to a lack of genuine and lasting friendships. Paradoxically, the behavior of young adults during the recent COVID-19 pandemic reflects both the individualism and need for belonging. Young people flaunt the recommendations to wear

34. Reed, "Book for None?," 8.

35. For example, Jesus instructs his followers to "deny self" (Matt 16:24) and "serve others" (Mark 9:35). Likewise, Paul exhorts the early Christians to "consider others better than oneself" (Phil 2:1) and to "look not only one's own interests but those of others" (Phil 4:23).

36. Wuthnow, *Loose Connections*.

37. Gallagher, "Christian Identity," 146.

masks in public and continue to congregate in bars and restaurants in large numbers. While Twenge is unsure whether religion will fulfill the need for community,[38] I would argue that building authentic relationships in the early stages of pre-evangelization might awaken a latent and unacknowledged human need for friendship.

Epistemological and Phenomenological Implications

The above characteristics may justifiably lead to changes in the epistemological and phenomenological frameworks related to spirituality and religion. Epistemology refers to a way of understanding and explaining how an individual knows what is known.[39] Phenomenology may be defined as how an individual becomes conscious of or interprets an event or experience. For example, consider how, for previous generations of young adults, knowledge of God and faith was often transmitted by external information or dogmatically proclaimed through metanarratives and practices passed down through family, tribe, or culture. When these sources of knowledge are either absent or deemed unbelievable, young adults may come to an awareness of knowledge of God and religion primarily through their individual experience. Nebreda argues that difficulties and obstacles which hinder dialogue with a nonbeliever are less intellectually based and more existential and pre-suppositional prejudices.[40] In contrast to a cerebral explanation of religious facts, Emery White proposes that the initial approach toward unchurched young adults might better be more experientially based; thus, young adults progress in the spiritual journey from first feeling into thinking, rather than the other way around.[41] Kinnaman and Lyons confirm that young adults are attracted to spirituality and faith because of overwhelmingly subjective emotional and experiential factors.[42]

In the context of a religious conversion, a phenomenological perspective acknowledges that an individual will approach a specific experience uniquely according to one's state of consciousness or being, which may

38. Twenge, *iGen*, 142.

39. Crotty, *Foundations of Social Research*, 3.

40. Nebreda, *Kerygma*, 82.

41. White, *Rethinking the Church*, 61.

42. Kinnaman and Lyons, *unChristian*, 70. Interestingly, they note that both young adult Christians (67 percent) and "outsiders" (69 percent) cite that faith or spirituality must "feel right to them personally."

include genetics, culture, previous experiences, and physiological state. Thus, an experience which is perceived by one person to be an encounter with the transcendent named as God may be attributed by another to mere awe at nature. Such an awareness may prompt the use of a new vocabulary which is less reliant upon or even avoids religious jargon. Generic language such as "silence," "meaning," "values," and "transformation" (as opposed to worship, truth, or conversion) may be utilized to express or seek to understand the other without jumping to an immediate correlation to Christianity or another religious tradition.

American Cultural Characteristics

Certain American cultural characteristics, including a longstanding tradition of religious freedom, separation of church and state, considerable religious diversity, and secularization may also have influenced young adults' religious attitudes. While the United States was founded on the constitutional ideals of religious freedom, data from a study by Stark and Finke hints that colonial America was probably not as stereotypically pious as nostalgia might lead its citizens to believe.[43] Rather, the practice of religion and reason were sometimes considered dichotomous. Historian Christopher Dawson observed that "American society derived [its spiritual] force from the religious idealism of sectarian Protestantism and its principles from the eighteenth century ideology of Natural Rights and rational Enlightenment."[44] Thus, American expressions of faith and those who profess some measure of faith are still powerfully shaped by and accommodate easily to social norms of reasonableness.[45]

A foundational principle in the US Constitution is the separation of church and state. Berger argues this means that Americans faced the challenge of religious pluralism from the start. Rather than follow a state-imposed religion, an individual needed to make choices. Thus, religion was voluntary from the beginning.[46] Today, Americans have greater and more varied opportunities to participate in the religion of their choice or practice no religion at all.[47] Interestingly, Jozef Ratzinger proposes that

43. Stark and Finke, *Churching of America*, 25.
44. Dawson, *Understanding Europe*, 128–48.
45. Wuthnow, *God Problem*, viii, ix, 3, 26.
46. Mathewes, "Interview with Peter Berger," 156.
47. Lipset, *Continental Divide*, 75.

this principle has positively influenced the practice of religion within the United States to the extent that religion has not diminished to the level of that in Western Europe.[48]

A notable outgrowth of this principle is the 1963 prohibition of public (or government supported) schools in the United States from teaching religion, although teaching about religion in a secular context is permitted.[49] While the enrollment in public schools has remained steady since that time, from 1963–64 to 1991–92 enrollment in Catholic schools has decreased 55 percent.[50] This means that, in the absence of a tribal religious faith or practice, three generations in the United States have not grown up with daily exposure to a faith or understanding of basic facts about religion.

If faith (in terms of content, practice, and assent) is not being handed down to successive generations, then I predict that the pattern will likely continue. Hervieu-Léger defines this phenomenon as "collective memory" or the shared pooled knowledge and memories of two or more members of a social group.[51] For example, when both parents and grandparents of the current generation of young adults have not actively practiced and transmitted the faith, then there is no memory or language being passed down to the subsequent generations. Hence, each subsequent generation becomes less open and disposed.

Reed notes that, according to the 2013 Public Research on Religion Institute report, many of the current young adult "nones" are second generation "nones" because they grew up in nonreligious households and have merely continued that nonreligious position.[52] Sr. Kathleen Mitchell, a Franciscan sister who works with young adults in Chicago, indicates that many young adults today have not been raised in any faith tradition.[53] Twenge's research affirms that more teens (and hence, tomorrow's young adults) are being raised by nonreligious parents.[54] In my own research with young adult

48. "Cardinal Ratzinger Commends."

49. The United States Supreme Court decided in the case of School District of Abington Township, Pennsylvania. vs. Schempp, 374 US 203 (1963) that any state-sponsored promotion of prayer or other devotional practice was prohibited in alignment with the Establishment Clause of the First Amendment in the United States Constitution. The Establishment Clause constrains the US government from involving itself in religious matters.

50. Snyder, "120 Years of American Education," 49.

51. Hervieu-Léger, *Religion as a Chain of Memory*.

52. Reed, "Book for None?," 5.

53. Mitchell, "Are They Finding a Place?," 77.

54. Twenge, *Generation Me*, 43.

catechumens,[55] which will be discussed in chapter 9, I discovered that many parents, both those who grew up in a faith tradition and those who did not, are allowing their children to make their own decisions about religion rather than steer them into a particular set of beliefs.

Occasionally, the American media links the decrease in religious attendance to a growing secularization, which may be defined as the decline in the authority or power of religious organizations. However, several scholars dispute this theory, claiming that religion is not on the decline because, in contrast to Western Europe, the United States tends to have higher religious participation.[56] For example, Durkheim contended that while a culture may become more secularized, it would not necessarily become desacralized.[57] Taylor suggests that those who have grown up in a postmodern period feel a kind of "cross-pressure," nostalgically holding on to the sacred while at the same time chafing against the so-called rules of religion and doggedly maintaining their own individual right to choose.[58] Curiously, the development of a growing number of terms used by young adults, such as "spiritual but not religious," indicate a less rigid and more fluid, nuanced understanding of the practice of faith and spirituality.

Young Adults and the Church

Young adulthood is often a time of flux, accompanied by a series of transitions, life markers, or rites of passage. Traditionally, some of these rites in contemporary American culture have included moving out of the parental home, attending college, getting a full-time job, paying one's own expenses, getting married, and having children. Smith proposes four macro-level social transformations which have affected young adults in recent decades: (1) growth in higher education, (2) delay in marriage,

55. A catechumen is "an unbaptized person who is preparing for full initiation" into the Catholic Church, while a candidate is an individual who has "already been baptized in another Church or ecclesial community" and who seeks to become incorporated into the Catholic Church. Both catechumens and candidates may participate in the RCIA.

56. For example, Wuthnow, *God Problem*, 2, 20–28; Taylor, *Secular Age*, 524–28; Stark and Finke, *Churching of America*, 16, 19.

57. Durkheim, *Elementary Forms*, 474–76. Because the sacred is dependent on the society or culture which attaches meaning to it, new expressions of the sacred or the transcendent could include certain rituals, public ceremonies, and gatherings such as sporting events.

58. Taylor, *Secular Age*, 544.

(3) instability in American and global economy, and (4) parents willing to extend financial and other support to children into their twenties and early thirties.[59] But Wuthnow claims that, due to longer life expectancies, people are reaching their midpoint in life later; thus, young adults are delaying these developmental tasks.[60]

This delay may impact young adults' interest in the practice of a religious faith. For example, marriage, children, and religion seem to be intrinsically linked. Wuthnow suggests that religious involvement is influenced more by whether people are married, when they get married, whether they have children, and how many children they have than almost anything else.[61] Smith further argues that the postponement of marriage and children is strongly correlated with reduced practice of religion in America, because religion is perceived as a factor of "settling down" and directed toward one's future.[62] Thus, it may not be surprising when 72 percent of Catholic converts (both unbaptized and those baptized in another faith) cite marriage as an important reason for their switch in faith.[63] At the same time, a 2008 CARA study indicated that among adult converts, 48 percent were between the ages of 18 and 29, which could suggest that young adulthood may be a ripe time for conversion.[64] At the same time, Twenge found that, even after having their own children, participation of young adults in their thirties in religious activities is still lower than that of previous generations.[65]

Rather than "settling down," many young adults "are still sorting out what their purpose in life might be." And yet, this "purpose" is less an existential and more a pragmatic search for what one ought to be doing with

59. USCCB, *Sons and Daughters*; Smith and Snell, *Souls in Transition*, 34, 75, 5–6.

60. Wuthnow, *God Problem*, 20. While many American young adults have traditionally chosen a life partner and begun having children at this stage, three-quarters (75 percent) of surveyed young adults have never married, compared with only 43 percent of the Silent generation, 52 percent of Boomers, and 67 percent of Gen Xers at the same ages (Pew Research Center, "Millennials: A Portrait", 11). Further, contemporary young adults were more likely to be living with a parent, cohabiting with a partner, or living with a roommate than other generations at the same stage in life (ibid., 12).

61. Wuthnow, *God Problem*, 17.

62. Smith and Snell, *Souls in Transition*, 79–80.

63. Pew Research Center, "Faith in Flux." Interestingly, the response with the second highest percentage was "found a religion [one] liked more" (68 percent). The study seemed to indicate that, unlike conversions to Catholicism, few conversions to other faith traditions were due to marriage.

64. Gray and Perl, *Sacraments Today*, 25.

65. Twenge, *Generation Me*, 43.

one's life.[66] The busyness of establishing oneself, whether in a new location or job or finding new friends, may distract young adults from focusing on religious and spiritual interests and getting involved in a faith community. Exposure to new social groups in the college dormitory or workplace may also challenge the practice of childhood religious beliefs. I would also suggest that because young adults are choosing to delay marriage or even opt out of getting married in lieu of living together with a partner, the motivation for conversion becomes even more subjective.

Faith in Flux

Belief and spirituality are also in flux as young adults seek to form their own identity apart from their family or native tribe. These movements might even be expected. Among James Fowler's six stages of faith development, the Individuative-Reflective faith stage falls within the traditional period of young adulthood. During this stage, young adults may become suspicious of conventional religious beliefs and take on responsibility for discovering their own truths.[67] The exodus from the church for many young adults who have grown up in a religious family or who have been given a solid Christian education may be partially attributed to this theory. Exposure to new ideas from peer groups and the desire for independence, with support from cultural factors mentioned above, fuel the departure.

But if young adults are leaving the Church for many of these reasons, what about those "native nones" who themselves are now exposed to new beliefs in the form of Christianity? If Fowler's hypothesis is correct, one of the challenges of pre-evangelization is both to recognize and honor this stage, while at the same time to respond to the questions that arise in the person's mind and heart.

This period of intense self-focus may create a rather unsettled state for young adults. The busyness of life often relegates the religious or spiritual search to the background unless stimulated by an outside event. After college, young adults have very little institutional support for navigating these major life tasks. It is not surprising, therefore, that they turn to answers from the surrounding culture, technology (and in particular, social media), and themselves, a quest which deepens the tendency toward an individualistic spirituality.

66. Smith and Snell, *Souls in Transition*, 53; cf. Twenge, *iGen*, 167–69.
67. Fowler, *Stages of Faith*, 174–83.

Don't Preach to Me

Over the past five years, I have observed a general trend of heightened sensitivity among American young adults who feel distressed over messages or information which may give offense to another. This phenomenon could likely extend to and include any verbal statement that seems to indicate a hegemony of Christian thought against other sets of belief or nonbelief. A February 2019 report released by Barna Group stated that "almost half of millennials (47 percent) agree at least somewhat that it is wrong to share one's personal beliefs with someone of a different faith in hopes that they will one day share the same faith." Further, 40 percent feel that even a disagreement about beliefs is associated with judgment.[68] So while young adults may express the right to religious freedom in concept, at the same time they reject speech that is considered aggressive. Stephen Prothero remarked that his young adult students could accept "respectful" conversations, but they are allergic to "argument."[69] Therefore, evangelization and other associated words are sometimes viewed or identified synonymously and in a pejorative sense with proselytism.

In the current papacy, Francis has spoken multiple times against proselytism as a coercive, manipulative means of spreading the message of the gospel. Above all, he insists that evangelization is about attraction and witness, which includes getting to know another, listening, and improving knowledge of the other and their environment.

While sincere Christians may not need to declare a "trigger warning" in every instance before sharing their beliefs, believers may need to have a greater awareness of how expressions of difference, together with professed exclusivity of truth, may be equated with intolerance and privilege. A premature proclamation of the *kerygma* could be repelling and have the undesired effect of pushing the unchurched young adult away from exploring the faith.

An Unwelcoming Church

Many young adults express negativity around their experiences with religious institutions.[70] They do not experience a sense of welcome at a

68. Barna Group, "Almost Half."

69. Prothero, *God Is Not One*, 4.

70. Barna Group and Cornerstone Knowledge Network, *Making Space for Millennials*. Statistics and findings can also be found at "What Millennials Want."

religious service or Mass. Instead, they find belonging and community more often in nonreligious groups and activities.[71] This phenomenon may be a self-fulfilling prophecy: if a young adult enters a church building with certain expectations and sees no or few others of the same age, or lacks an affinity or resonance with those in the community, he or she may avoid the church in the future.

Some American young adults feel disinclined toward religious institutions because of their perceptions, right or wrong. Among several reasons cited in Kinnaman and Lyons' study were a lack of comfort to share their deepest questions, concerns, or doubts within a church setting.[72] In particular, young adults felt their theological questions were either left unanswered or answered simplistically.[73] Parishes "all too often, [have] a tendency to provide prepackaged answers and ready-made solutions [to young adults] without allowing their real questions to emerge."[74] Only 34 percent of surveyed young adult "outsiders" believe that Christians really care about them individually, preferring to cut to the chase and get the quick conversion; as opposed to 64 percent of Christians who felt outsiders would view them as genuine.[75]

Further, many young adults think churches are repressive, especially with regards to sexuality; they are uncomfortable with the so-called exclusivist message of the gospel; they sense tension between the claims of Christianity and science; they percieve Christians to be simultaneously judgmental and yet hypocritical and to lack practical application to real life. Such beliefs have been less influenced by the secular media and more by negative personal experiences and relationships with other churches and Christians.[76] In contrast, Twenge's research found that young adults seek positive messages from churches about happiness, hope, and becoming a better person.[77]

While I do not suggest that churches reduce their theology or message to a lowest common denominator type of faith, pre-evangelization needs to honestly address these concerns.

---

71. Smith and Snell, *Souls in Transition*, 286, 152; *IL*, 21.

72. Kinnaman, *You Lost Me*; see also Mitchell, "Are They Finding a Place?" 75.

73. Mercadante, "Seeker Next Door," 30.

74. *IL*, 8.

75. Kinnaman and Lyons, *unChristian*, 66–67.

76. Kinnaman and Lyons, *unChristian*, 27–28, 31–32, 34.

77. Twenge, *iGen*, 140.

Technology and Young Adults

Young adults communicate differently than generations in the past. Socially, they have been influenced by an explosion in the use of technology and are often known as "digital natives," having grown up with computer screens and smartphones in their hands. Notably, when asked the defining characteristics of their generation from others, young adults emphasized the use of technology.[78] Pew cites 88 percent of young adults aged 18–29 years use online social media.[79] Muldoon believes many young adults interact in a virtual world to assuage their loneliness yet find a lack of depth and authenticity in online relationships.[80] The trend is likely to continue; Twenge comments that the current generation of young adults has been shaped even more by the smartphone and the rise of social media.[81] Social media includes not only websites which serve as social networking, such as Facebook, Twitter, and Instagram, but also a variety of websites, blogs, online videos, and digital tools like text messaging. All of these may potentially serve as powerful tools for pre-evangelization to young adults.

Vogt suggests that new media can be promising forums for digital evangelization by facilitating dialogue through connection and conversation.[82] As early as 1990, John Paul II hailed mass media and emerging forms of communication as a kind of virtual Areopagus, referring to Paul's sermon engaging the men of Athens. At a World Communications Day in 2009, Benedict XVI called the Catholic Church to embrace the "digital continent" in terms of its opportunity to become a forum for witness among young people.[83] As an example, Robert Barron, an American Catholic bishop who regularly posts short videos on YouTube, claims he has successfully engaged young men by disputing a number of so-called "heresies," obstacles, or arguments against the faith during online conversations.[84] Schneider offers three illustrations of the use of digital evangelization to young adults, which includes Twitter feeds featuring a narrative describing real life struggles and

---

78. Pew Research Center, "Millennials: A Portrait," 5–6, 13–14; *IL*, 34–35.

79. Pew Research Center, "Social Media Use in 2018."

80. Muldoon, *Seeds of Hope*, 138.

81. Twenge, *iGen*.

82. Vogt, *Church and New Media*, 17.

83. Benedict XVI, "New Technologies."

84. Vogt, *Church and New Media*, 17–19. Vogt works with Barron in his Word on Fire Catholic ministry, which includes an online component.

faith (which adds authenticity), beauty in photographs through Instagram posts, as well as online videos.[85]

Despite these examples, conversing with young adults through social media may not be the panacea for which faith leaders may be hoping. While young adults enjoy the ability to communicate instantaneously with others around the globe, they are simultaneously exposed to an influx of various ideas and opinions that may reduce the value of the Christian message to only one among other equals. If young adults are interested in religion or spirituality, they can easily conduct research on the internet, where they have access to unlimited information; the pervasiveness of digital "fake news," however, may make their search for truth problematic.[86] Many create a hybrid religious identity, picking and choosing what suits them. Spitzer argues that the constant distraction of technology and media makes it difficult for young adults to find the time to ask the difficult existential questions, which may prompt conversion.[87] And, in their study of 560 young adults, Bobkowski and Pearce found that "social media users rarely disclose much about religion in their online profiles and, when they do, their disclosures tend to be brief and superficial."[88]

Openings for Young Adults

All this negativity toward the church does not mean contemporary young adults are an unreachable audience. Phan suggests that, far from despairing the relativism, subjectivism, and skepticism of postmodernity, to offer an opportunity for Christians to humbly and respectfully dialogue with others who disagree and who together seek the truth.[89] This form of conversational evangelization emerges strongly in the Second Vatican Council documents and continues to be encouraged in papal writings; some Protestant theologians are also now awakening to its benefits in terms of reaching the contemporary young adult.

On one level, Smith and Snell note that young adults simply do not feel a need for God, faith, worship, and prayer; religion is not a "life driver." They do not actively seek or take much initiative in pursuit of the spiritual.

85. Schneider, "Applying Six Offline Models."
86. *IL*, 34–35, 54.
87. Molloy, "Four Things."
88. Bobkowski and Pearce, "Baring Their Souls," 744–62.
89. Phan, "Evangelization in a Culture," 7.

Moreover, faith is generally not "something most [young adults] talk about with their friends or romantic partners."[90] Yet, young adults seem generally happy and open to talk about religion. If, as the document from the 2018 Synod on Young People claims, young adults are "major seekers of meaning, and are intrigued and motivated to action by anything that is in tune with their quest to give value to their lives," then spirituality as a conduit to meaning-making may be a possible route.[91] As Smith explains:

> Religion might be irrelevant to emerging adults as a group, but that does not mean they are hostile to it. Many are intrigued. They want to talk about it. Many who were raised nonreligious feel culturally deprived of this big part of life. Many churches seem to think that nonreligious young people are all atheistic like Richard Dawkins, but they aren't. They're aware that they don't know much about religious tradition. Many want a conversation. If churches don't make an effort to engage, it won't happen.[92]

Kinnaman adds that some nonbelieving young adults have never even thought about becoming Christian.[93] This suggests that some conversations in the earliest stages of evangelization may need to become more intentional and direct. Engaging a young adult in a discussion about faith, religion, or Jesus Christ may not necessarily evoke a negative response, as may be anticipatorily perceived.

But because young adults are not often actively seeking and far less expecting such conversations in a church setting, the locus may need to shift to the secular environment. Faith leaders cannot expect young adults simply to show up at the local Mass or worship service. Nor do promotional events aimed at their age demographic seem to attract them. Unchurched young adults seem impervious to traditional advertising by churches, such as direct mailings, television, billboard, or radio messaging, to get them in the door.[94] Such advertising is suspiciously viewed as a kind of marketing ploy or as a mask for an agenda.

90. Smith and Snell, *Souls in Transition*, 144, 154, 186, 296.

91. *IL*, 7, 106; many young adults cannot articulate the meaning of their life or connect their everyday life to transcendence.

92. "Young Souls in Transition."

93. Kinnaman and Lyons, *unChristian*, 49.

94. Hill, "Missing the Signs," 29; "Five Trends Among Unchurched." Kinnaman and Lyons found that 71 percent of young adults who made a personal (or, as termed, "born again") decision to believe in Jesus Christ were influenced by a witness, namely a parent, friend, other relative, or teacher, and through conversations and prayer; far fewer of these

Conversations also need to be both sincerely initiated and based upon an exchange of ideas. Young adults do not want to be pressured or cornered into conversations in a way that is insincere or disingenuous; in other words, no "hype" or "schtick."[95] At the same time, many nonbelieving young adults perceive that Christians are unwilling to engage in dialogue and are more concerned about persuading the other with the "correctness" of their own view.[96] A frequent phrase used in young adult vocabulary is the "safe space," which often refers to a specified physical location where persons can feel emotionally secure. Therefore, conversations may need to be conducted in "safe spaces" where both Christians and nonbelievers share views and feelings without judging another's opinion.

Another possible point of entry is through stimulating the experience of the transcendent. Spitzer observes that nonbelieving young adults share "no sense of ultimate dignity and meaning and transcendence,"[97] a possible response to a rampant cultural materialism, which diminishes or denies the spiritual. The 2018 Synod on Young People affirms that the "sacred is often quite separate" from daily life.[98] Both Smith and Mercadante believe young adults are open to experiencing a kind of a higher power.[99] Taylor seems to connect a sense of "fullness" with transcendence through an external, unanticipated, and unexplained experience or event, which jars or disrupts the individual outside of the rationality of one's mind.[100] If young adults do not sense a need for "fullness" or transcendence is not explicitly acknowledged, then the possibility may need to be awakened and experienced.

In response to the hyper-individualism and disincarnated relationships on social media, many pastors say that contemporary young adults seek a faith community where they experience cultural relevance, authenticity, connection to social concerns, and access to close relationships and community. Such longings may resonate as an antidote from eroded familial and friendship ties. On the other hand, Pew reports that religiously

were influenced by a personal invitation to a church service or other church-sponsored event. Kinnaman and Lyons, *unChristian*, 68.

95. Kinnaman and Lyons, *unChristian*, 66.

96. Kinnaman and Lyons, *unChristian*, 31.

97. Molloy, "Four Things." In the 2018 Synod on Young People, young adult seminarians and religious seem to indicate that the Church should be more mystical, offering glimpses of transcendence; see *IL*, 72.

98. *IL*, 29.

99. Smith and Snell, *Souls in Transition*, 144, 159; Mercadante, "Seeker Next Door," 33.

100. Taylor, *Secular Age*, 5–6, 728–31 Taylor labels this a kind of conversion.

unaffiliated adults in general tend to place far less importance on sharing one's beliefs and values with a community while Smith and Snell found that young adults generally sought belonging and community in nonreligious groups and activities.[101]

What does this mean for young adults and the kerygmatic message of Christianity, traditionally associated with evangelization? Possibly that religious pluralism, in combination with a skepticism toward absolute truth and the Christian metanarrative, as well as an extreme focus on the individual and experience, may leave nonbelieving young adults questioning any ready-made answers promoted by an institutional or denominational faith. It may also explain the tendency for young adults to veer toward an individualistic spirituality. In other words, young adults may not be ready or able to comprehend the core Christian message about salvation without acknowledging the existence of a God, sin, and the love of God for humanity expressed through the God-man, Jesus Christ.

In the absence of a tribal faith, young adults may have absorbed many subtle or overt messages about Christianity through friends, a religious school, and even the surrounding culture. However, young adults today have witnessed and experienced different political and social events which may have eroded their confidence in structures of authority, including the church. Culturally, the postmodern influences of secularism (defined as the separation of the state and religion), materialism (which diminishes or denies the spiritual or transcendent), and relativism (which questions or denies universal truths) may have not given young adults a positive context in which to consciously explore religious faith. Kinnaman and Lyons observe that "Christianity," used either as a noun or adjective, is viewed more with reference to a brand than as a faith and the perception of the brand is negative.[102] Christianity may be associated with extremism, intolerance, and narrow-mindedness, among other pejoratives.

Spitzer, a Catholic priest who both ministered and taught at Gonzaga University, noted that religion is perceived by young adult nonbelievers as a "crutch" for those who cannot handle the difficulties of life; believing in Christ could therefore be considered a weakness in character. Young adults often struggle with how a "loving" God could allow suffering in the physical world. Finally, Spitzer argues that young adults lack the ability to provide a

---

101. Pew Research Center, "'Nones' on the Rise," 55; Smith and Snell, *Souls in Transition*, 152.

102. Kinnaman and Lyons, *unChristian*, 221.

cogent response to a secular media that portrays Jesus as myth. He proposes that a kind of apologetics allows Christians to defend the faith intellectually and intelligently and "reconstruct God."[103] This type of pre-evangelization may also dispel some of the misperceptions which nonbelievers hold against Christians and predispose them toward future dialogue.

Without a religious foundation in either the family or through the academic environment, Muldoon claims that many young adults have a "theological illiteracy" and have not been exposed to the wealth of knowledge within the Christian heritage and may hold a misunderstanding of the Catholic tradition.[104] In addition, Kinnaman and Lyons suggest that many Christians speak about Scripture at a level in which others cannot understand because American society does not have a background knowledge of the Bible.[105] If young adults do not understand the typical vocabulary used in a soteriological narrative about Christ, the kerygmatic proclamation may likely sound mythical, illogical, or irrational.

Another example of a possible obstacle with a premature proclamation of the *kerygma* is the perception of the term "sin" and one's own personal responsibility. Twenge argues that some young adults possess a strong sense of externality, meaning that they do not believe they are in control of their circumstances; however, she claims this may also lead to a victim mentality and a declining belief in personal responsibility.[106] Van Dop's follow-up interviews with adult converts noted a lack of emphasis on sin or use of other traditional religious language when recounting their preconversion experience.[107] If this is true, it is possible that young adults may not attribute a personal, moral responsibility to their own acts and thus have difficulty in understanding the concept of sin and the need for an external figure or God to save them.

The above factors seem to support an initial preparation or pre-evangelization before nonbelieving young adults are ready to hear and respond to an explicit message about Jesus Christ. What is this pre-evangelization and how does it relate to evangelization? In the next chapter, I will explore the historical development of evangelization within the Catholic Church and introduce how the term "pre-evangelization" evolved in its original context.

103. Molloy, "Four Things."

104. Muldoon, *Seeds of Hope*, 85, 94.

105. Kinnaman and Lyons, *unChristian*, 209.

106. Twenge, *Generation Me*, 182, 196–99, 185.

107. Van Dop, "Connecting to God," 172.

3

A Brief History of Pre-Evangelization

WHILE AMERICAN CATHOLICS ARE slowly becoming more familiar (even if still slightly confused and uncomfortable) with the New Evangelization, outside of a narrow group of academics in the study of catechetics, they are very likely ignorant of the term "pre-evangelization." The term itself did not even emerge in the catechetical circles of the Catholic Church until the 1950s. Given the vast outreaches associated with historical missions in the Far East and the Americas, this might seem surprising. However, the action of proclaiming the gospel message was primarily associated in the past with the word "mission." In fact, until 1955, the word "evangelization" was scarcely found and perhaps even avoided in Catholic theological literature because it was considered a "Protestant term."[1]

This chapter will provide a brief history of pre-evangelization prior to Vatican II, beginning with its scriptural roots. The proclamation and transmission of the faith often became intertwined with colonialism and indoctrination before transitioning toward a more kerygmatic approach. New circumstances in the mid-twentieth century, including changes in the mission field and the secularization of Western countries, prompted a renewed interest on how to attract and predispose the nonbeliever before the actual proclamation of the gospel and catechesis.

---

1. Gorski, "From 'Mission,'" 3.

Evangelization in the New Testament

The Catholic term "evangelization" and the corresponding Protestant term "evangelism" both derive from the Greek noun *euangelion* (meaning "good news") and the verb *euangelizomai*, which means to announce, proclaim, or bring good news. Mercadante claims that the noun was historically and culturally used to refer to someone who announced this "good news," likely the subject of a wedding or military victory.[2]

Scripturally, the foundation for evangelization is situated in the Gospel of Matthew when, before his ascension to heaven, Jesus charges his disciples to "Go, therefore, and make disciples of all nations (*ethne*), baptizing them in the name of the Father, Son, and Holy Spirit, teaching them to observe all that I commanded you" (Matt 28:19–20). A similar passage in Mark 16:15 gives a more message-driven directive to "Go into the whole world and proclaim the gospel to every creature." These passages imply both a movement away from the local community and a definite set of actions.

However, is Jesus' command within these Gospel passages exclusive or restricted to the overall Christian understanding of mission or evangelization? For example, the chapter of Matthew 25 appears to equate the person of Jesus with the poor and suffering. Jesus' own public ministry described in all four Gospels includes not only explicit preaching, but also acts of healing, forgiving, and feeding the crowds, implying both a vertical and horizontal dimension to evangelization. In the Book of Acts, Jesus' apostles seem to carry out this command through preaching, but also through dialogue with pagans and through service to the small Christian communities. Thus, the term "mission" in the Christian context can be broadly defined to encompass *kerygma* (proclamation), *koininia* (community), *diakonia* (service), and *martyria* (witness). Likewise, the terms "evangelization" and "mission" have both been associated with words such as preaching, conversion, gospel, Good News, and liberation.

My concern is that if Christians hold a traditional perspective or narrow definition of evangelization as proclamation of the *kerygma* only, then this meaning will limit how pre-evangelization is also understood. Yet while Scripture may give the reader some indication of a historical practice of evangelization which seems to be respectful of its surrounding cultures, the history of the Catholic Church and its method of spreading the *euangelion* since the 1500s may be judged to be less than Christ-like.

2. Mercadante, *Engaging a New Generation*, 101.

Evangelization Prior to Vatican II

The Roman Catholic Church does not exactly have a great track record with evangelization. Over the past five centuries, the Church's method of evangelization has evolved from a style of proclamation as imposition or even subjugation toward a proclamation as proposition.[3] Catholic missionary activity from the mid-1500s to the mid-1900s was primarily directed to non-Christians in areas of the world being colonized by the European and American states.[4] The Spanish priest Bartolomé de las Casas recounts horrific narratives describing the widespread violence and enslavement of the native American peoples under the pretext of teaching them "the Holy Catholic Faith."[5] At times, missionaries from religious orders such as the Franciscans forced baptisms and conversions upon the native American populations.[6] Pathrapankal and Gorski assert that the emphasis on making disciples and baptizing natives was motivated not so much from a commitment to Christ, but rather from a commitment to increasing converts to one's own denomination and for the wealth of the colonizing country.[7] However, Benedict XVI seems to mitigate the gravity of this behavior by suggesting that missionaries of this era may have been compelled by their belief in the absolute necessity of baptism for salvation.[8]

As a reaction to the Reformation, the Catholic Church adopted a defensive or fortress mentality toward any methodology or belief that hinted of Protestantism.[9] For example, while Protestants over-emphasized the role of an individual's faith (*sola fide,* meaning "by faith alone") for salvation, the post-Reformation understanding of faith by the Catholic Church centered on both content and verbal profession of doctrine. Dulles describes the primary approach to catechesis between the Council of Trent and the Second Vatican Council as doctrinal and moral teaching, along with providing an apologetic-style defense of the Catholic faith against Protestant

---

3. In John Paul II, *Redemptoris Missio,* 39, he states, "The Church proposes; she imposes nothing." However, I would argue that this statement was made in light of a new paradigm for missionary activity after the Second Vatican Council, which championed both religious freedom and inculturation.

4. Gorski, "From 'Mission,'" 2.

5. De las Casas, *History of the Indies,* 110.

6. Vidmar, *Catholic Church,* 243–46.

7. Pathrapankal, *Time and History,* 40; Gorski, "From 'Mission,'" 2.

8. Servais, "Intervista al Papa emerito Benedetto XVI," 5.

9. Hill, *Ongoing Renewal of Catholicism,* 116.

beliefs.[10] Nebreda suggests the Church shifted from a patristic understanding of faith as a personal, existential sense of commitment and trust toward a semi-Pelagian understanding of faith where the human person is saved through good actions.[11]

An example of this catechetical hermeneutic in the American context is the use of the Baltimore Catechism, published in the United States in 1885. Written in a question-and-answer format, this publication educated generations of American children who memorized texts, thus forming well-educated students in the content of the Catholic faith, including its moral and liturgical demands, but not necessarily those who understood their faith to include a personal relationship with Jesus.[12] As Avery Dulles points out, catechized young persons were assumed to come to an eventual understanding of these memorized truths later in life.[13]

However, the winds were shifting in terms of the method in which the faith was best passed down to the next generation. In the mid-to-late 1800s, John Henry Newman challenged the prevailing theology of faith as merely a notional assent toward a real assent. According to Newman, a notional assent refers to one's acceptance of the nature of another based on the hearsay, experience, or authority of another party; in contrast, real assent refers to one's ability to understand and accept the nature of an object or another subject as it is personally experienced and known by the subject.[14] Perhaps desiring to return to the original patristic understanding of faith, Newman advocated the individual's personal assent (the *actus fidei*, or "act of faith") as the integral component, emphasizing less the cognitive content of belief or even belief based upon another's experience. Further, Newman encouraged the use of the illative sense, which is the

---

10. Dulles, *Evangelization for Third Millennium*, 103.

11. Nebreda, *Kerygma*, 8–9.

12. Dulles, *Evangelization for Third Millennium,* 104, cites that the method of memorization used in the Baltimore Catechism "presupposed that students had previously been evangelized, but often this was not the case . . . [it] produced not a few unevangelized but well-catechized Catholics." Mongoven, *Prophetic Spirit,* 4, states that this catechetical publication was neither "christocentric, trinitarian or biblical."

13. Dulles, *Evangelization for Third Millennium*, 103.

14. As John Henry Newman states, "Real apprehension, then, may be pronounced stronger than notional, because things, which are its objects, are confessedly more impressive and affective than notions, which are the objects of notional." The entire section on real vs. notional assent can be found in ch. 4 in Newman, *Essay in Aid.*

ability to reflect on one's concrete experiences with the external world and thus arrive at the conclusion of a transcendent beyond.[15]

Hearkening back to the praxis of the early Church, several early twentieth-century theologians had advocated a renewal and reform of both the content and method of the transmission of the faith. Against a purely doctrinally-focused catechesis, Josef Jungmann and his student Johannes Hofinger argued for a recentering of the core content of the faith as the *kerygma,* or the explicit Christocentric proclamation of the gospel.[16] In contrast to a method focused on rote memorization of facts, Joseph Colomb sought to move catechesis from a purely intellectual act or acquisition of knowledge of the content of the faith to include the critical component of the will and affections (precipitating the *actus fidei*) in the one being evangelized or catechized. Colomb felt that the content should include Scripture, liturgy, doctrine, and "human experience."[17] Jungmann argued against a passive and habitual "unconscious Christianity" which was narrowly reduced and focused upon unconnected facts and rules. Within this ritualistic practice, he felt that prayer and morality had become separated from the essence of the faith, which is a relationship with Jesus Christ. Rather, the goal should be a "conscious Christianity" or an active faith, based upon individuals' personal conviction, which enlivens them to participate in and practice that faith and to advance the kingdom of God.[18] The purpose of such approaches was to reunify the content of the faith with the liturgy as well as daily experiences of life, thereby eliciting personal acts of faith. The kerygmatic approach relied on a deductive method, meaning that instructors in religious education began with the assumed facts of faith and then moved to human experience. They primarily lectured to their student audience and aimed at transferring facts.[19]

Feedback from Catholic missionaries' experiences with non-Christians in the non-Western world, however, seemed to indicate that native people were becoming more resistant and perhaps even impervious to the

15. See ch. 9 in Newman, *Essay in Aid.*

16. Among many texts by the authors, see Jungmann, *Frohbotschaft und Glaubensverkundigung.* The goal was less the acquisition of knowledge through theology but a transformation of life toward holiness through proclamation. Also, Hofinger and Buckley, *Good News.*

17. Mongoven, *Prophetic Spirit,* 50–51.

18. Jungmann, *Pastoral Liturgy,* 325–34. According to Jungmann, "conscious Christianity" goes beyond the "purely intellectual apologetic argument" (ibid., 330); the individual knows why he believes the content and has a personal stake in it.

19. Pollefeyt, "Reader: Course Didactics," 30.

proclamation of the kerygmatic message. In addition, formerly Christianized regions like France had experienced an extensive de-Christianization, which prompted catechists to express the need for potential converts to receive psychological and sociological conditioning as preparation for a kerygmatic presentation of Christ.[20] Further, those in leadership roles within the Catholic Church recognized a trend that many adults baptized as children in Christianized countries were gradually leaving the practice of the faith.[21] These phenomena drew attention to the need for greater study on how to prepare the potential convert to become receptive to the message of Jesus.

In 1951, Pierre-Andre Liègè introduced the term "pre-evangelization" within the French publication *Catholicisme*. Liègè did not separate a distinct time period for pre-evangelization from evangelization *per se*. However, he stressed the importance of making the Gospel "accessible" and working within "men's [*sic*] own milieu," a perspective which served to undergird the promotion of inculturation within many Vatican II documents.[22] Hofinger, who inaugurated a series of international catechetical study weeks, expanded this view of pre-evangelization as the psychological preparation for growth in faith—it should "arouse interest" and "dispose" the person to hear and appreciate the message of God.[23]

During the third catechetical gathering in Bangkok, the term "pre-evangelization" was formally recognized.[24] For the first time in the history of catechetics, three stages in the conversion process which normally characterize the journey of the adult to faith were defined: pre-evangelization, evangelization, and catechesis proper. In this trifecta, pre-evangelization was noted as a necessary "stage of preparation for the *kerygma* which, taking man as he is and where he is, makes a human dialogue possible and awakens in him the sense of God, an indispensable element for opening his heart to the message." Evangelization as a specific second stage was identified precisely as the "*kerygma*" or "the dynamic heralding of the substance of the Christian message, having [as] its goal personal conversion or initial

20. Nebreda, "East Asian Study Week."

21. Nebreda, *Kerygma*, 46–47. Nebreda asserts that both Catholic and Protestant missionaries and theologians were beginning to question a purely kerygmatic approach to catechesis in the mission fields of Asia (ibid., 40–42).

22. Liègè, "Evangelization," col. 756–64.

23. These include Nijmegen (1959), Eichstatt (1960), Bangkok (1962), Katigondo (1964), Manila (1967), and Medellin (1968); Hofinger and Stone, *Pastoral Catechetics*, 148.

24. For a detailed description of the results of this catechetical conference, see Nebreda, "East Asian Study Week," 717–30.

acceptance of Christ as the Lord." Catechesis, in turn, was understood as a third phase which is based upon the previous two stages of conversion and which "systematically develops the message [heard or received] . . . with its goal . . . to initiate [the human person] into Christian life and build within him a Christian personality."[25]

Thus, influenced by theologians who advocated out of pastoral practice and experience, the Catholic Church had begun to broaden its understanding of the stages of growth in faith. A recognition of the need for pre-evangelization reflected the existence of a plurality and diversity of cultures and religious beliefs and their effect on the human person. Evangelization as proclamation acknowledged that, out of this plurality and diversity, the *kerygma* would need to be articulated according to the context and hermeneutic in which it was received, while at the same time not losing its essential salvific and transcendent components. Yet, evangelization would not stop after this initial proclamation but would seek to move the potential convert into a process of catechesis or teaching, culminating with incorporation into the Body of Christ (understood as the local parish community) through baptism and active participation into the life of the Church. Catechesis, by itself, would become more of a training or initiation into the practice of the faith within the parish and wider community as well as a strengthening of Christian identity.

These changes influenced the preparation for discussions held during the Second Vatican Council (1962–1965). Participants in the catechetical study weeks brought a missionary emphasis and sought to share their ideas with other Church leaders. In turn, the theological and pastoral insights of the Council were brought back to future catechetical sessions.[26] Thus, the sessions "represented an evolving series of focuses, each building on the insights of those preceding."[27]

25. Nebreda, *Kerygma*, viii. For a matrix on the three stages of the "kerygmatic approach" for the missions, see Nebreda, "East Asian Study Week."

26. Mongoven, *Prophetic Spirit*, 51.

27. Mongoven, *Prophetic Spirit*, 26.

4

Pre-Evangelization according to Alfonso Nebreda and Magisterial Documents

IN THE PREVIOUS CHAPTER, I discussed the origins and rationale for pre-evangelization. But pre-evangelization as understood by Fr. Alfonso Nebreda was written in the context of a non-Christian foreign mission environment during the early to mid-1900s. Is this still valid in the contemporary American context? In order to respond to this question, I wish to delve a bit deeper into the contributions of Fr. Nebreda on this initial stage of evangelization. I will also explore how pre-evangelization has become situated in magisterial teachings by the Catholic Church since the Second Vatican Council. Finally, I will discuss how the current pope Francis embodies many of the characteristics associated with pre-evangelization, particularly in his communications to young people.

Nebreda on Pre-Evangelization

I consider Fr. Alfonso Nebreda to be one of the few but most prolific writers on pre-evangelization. Nebreda (1925–2005) was a Jesuit priest who worked in missions in Japan for many years and had participated in the 1962 Bangkok Catechetical Study. Arguably, Nebreda's two books, *Why the Kergyma?* and *Kerygma in Crisis,* written during and after the Second Vatican Council, could be considered the primary works which both unpacked the rationale and provided a vision for pre-evangelization. Reflecting upon his experience in the missions as well as communications with priests ministering in France, Nebreda was convinced that the Church could no longer presume the home, school, or surrounding culture would be able to inculcate the basics in Christian catechesis, even in previously Christianized nations. He claimed it was futile "to try to discuss [religion] without first preparing the way" through a pre-evangelization.[1]

Nebreda begins with the reality of the nature and experience of the person as an individual. While evangelization narrowly defined by the Bangkok Study as "proclamation" should be clearly Christocentric, Nebreda proposes that pre-evangelization should be solidly anthropocentric. He encourages believers to move outside of their own worldview to both meet and respect persons as they are, and seek "to appreciate the position of [the] hearers—to see through their eyes and feel through their hearts."[2] This approach, I suggest, differs with a homogenous approach of evangelization which regards the person in a utilitarian fashion in which the immediate (and often expedient) goal is conversion to the Christian faith.

To illustrate his approach, Nebreda explains that the language used must be adapted and tailored toward the nonbeliever as the subject. He proposes that many priests were educated in a deductive mentality, meaning that overall concepts or precepts were accepted by the audience and out of these premises, conclusions were drawn. However, individuals were now being educated in an inductive manner, where the student begins with multiple hypotheses which could be compiled into a larger theory or narrative.[3] In other words, those who sought to evangelize by simply proclaiming the gospel message as a metanarrative could find their words falling on deaf ears.

Rather than trying to prove the self-evidence of the truth of Christianity, Nebreda suggests that the evangelizer encourage the nonbeliever to talk and ask questions in a kind of examination.[4] The purpose of this query is to provide the evangelizer with insight about the nonbeliever and, at the same time, to stimulate a dialogue. Dialogue can be about anything in which the evangelizer and nonbeliever discover as common ground. The ability to dialogue, Nebreda claims, initiates a relationship which leads to trust so the other feels comfortable revealing him or herself.[5] Rather than cognitive

---

1. Nebreda, *Kerygma*, 54.
2. Nebreda, *Kerygma*, 50–51, 53.
3. Nebreda, *Kerygma*, 52–53.
4. Nebreda, *Kerygma*, 106.
5. Nebreda, *Kerygma*, 54, 119.

hurdles, he believes the first "obstacles to dialogue with an unbeliever are not merely theoretical or intellectual, but rather total existential prejudices that put [Christians] in a doubtful light as persons."[6] For example, the non-believer may have experienced a negative interaction with a Christian or religion in general, which may lead them to prejudge the Christian believer or the Church as being insincere or dishonest.

Professing the ultimate freedom of the human person, Nebreda does not embrace a voluntarist position. This means that he does not insist that pre-evangelization must necessarily result in a religious conversion. He acknowledges the first movement of grace from God toward the human individual, but the individual retains free will to decide whether and how to respond. At the same time, Nebreda recognizes that the act of faith often needs an antecedent on the horizontal level; he defines the antecedent as a necessary condition, but not a cause for conversion.[7]

Based upon God's incarnational theology as revealed through Jesus Christ, the individual and collective witness is at the core of pre-evangelization on the horizontal level.[8] The authenticity and credibility of the witness is intrinsically tied to the receptivity of the eventual message. The act of faith, understood by Nebreda, becomes less a profession of content and more as a personal experience of, relationship with, and commitment to God as a Someone.[9] Perceiving the love of God through the relationship with the witness leads to the desire for knowledge of God.

Echoing John Henry Newman, Nebreda felt that faith needed to move beyond the intellect to the heart.[10] Thus, it may not be surprising that he expresses mixed support for the use of apologetics in pre-evangelization. On one hand, he stresses the importance of apologetics as a preparation of the *kerygma* and to avoid a purely emotionally based conversion.[11] Yet he opposes arguments about religion, including those based upon scientific evidence, as he believes these do not convince anyone.[12] Apologetics can

6. Nebreda, *Kerygma*, 120.

7. Nebreda, *Kerygma*, 105, 74, 78. As Nebreda writes, "We do not carry on pre-evangelization for the sake of pre-evangelization, but to prepare the way for Christ" (ibid., 104).

8. Nebreda, *Kerygma*, 116.

9. Nebreda, *Kerygma*, 12.

10. Nebreda, *Kerygma*, 18. Says Nebreda, "Newman . . . realized that the approach to faith is not intellectual but essentially moral, a problem therefore of the heart."

11. Nebreda, *Kerygma*, 48–49.

12. Nebreda, *Kerygma*, 58.

therefore be distinguished between objective, intellectual proofs for the faith versus subjective defenses which prepare the listener to be able to see the holy or transcendent within their own life and be open to the possibility for a future dialogue.[13]

Nebreda's commentary on the cultural landscape and his prescriptions are remarkably prophetic considering that he is writing within the environment of the late 1950s and early 1960s. In particular, he distinguishes three milieux for pre-evangelization, all of which are apropos for the pluralistic culture of American young adults today.[14] Nebreda's ideas are also distinctly echoed in Francis' papacy. For example, Nebreda suggests the attractiveness of witness is more important than words; within *Evangelii Gaudium*, Francis' overall theme is the impact of a joy-filled evangelizer which attracts others to the gospel.[15] In contrast, Christians are chastised for failing to exhibit behavior which would appeal to others and acting divisively with other Christians.[16] Both esteem the virtue of patience in evangelization; as Nebreda insists, "God's pedagogy does not follow a schedule."[17]

Pre-Evangelization Post-Vatican II

The documents which emerged from the Second Vatican Council (1962–1965) concretized the Catholic Church's understanding of mission, and thus evangelization, in terms of significance, responsibility, and praxis. A rough analysis of content, as Dulles explains, demonstrates the increasing importance of evangelization during the second half of the twentieth century:

13. Nebreda, *Kerygma*, 61–62.

14. Nebreda, *Kerygma*, 77.

15. Cf. Nebreda, *Kerygma*, 118–19; *EG*, 6. "Christians whose lives seem like Lent without Easter." Francis warns "an evangelizer must never look like someone who has just come back from a funeral!" (*EG*, 10).

16. Nebreda argues that Christians should "shine" but there is nothing shining in them; among other references. Nebreda, *Kerygma*, 86. Francis calls some Christians "sourpusses." *EG*, 85. Also, compare Nebreda, *Kerygma*, 86, with *EG*, 98–100, where Francis cites exclusivity, jealousy, and the desire for power among behaviors which serve to divide Christians.

17. Nebreda, *Kerygma*, 58. Nebreda lists the primary virtues associated with pre-evangelization, including sympathy and understanding, which rest upon patience, love, and a desire to see what is good and true in the lives of those to be evangelized. Nebreda, *Kergyma*, 106. Francis exhorts evangelizers to expect a lengthier process of conversion, which requires patience. *EG*, 24.

A simple word count indicates the profound shift in focus. Vatican I, which met from 1869–1870, used the term gospel (*evangelium*) only once and never used the terms evangelize and evangelization. Less than a century later, Vatican II mentioned the gospel 157 times and used the verb evangelize eighteen times and the noun evangelization thirty-one times. When it spoke of evangelization, Vatican II generally meant the proclamation of the basic Christian message of salvation through Jesus Christ.[18]

Thus, the stage was reset for a new understanding of what mission would look like for the Catholic Church in the mid-twentieth century and beyond. Conciliar documents, notably *Lumen Gentium, Ad Gentes,* and *Gaudium et Spes,* challenged the Church to view the secular world positively rather than defensively, to acknowledge differences between various cultures and religious beliefs, and to appreciate the presence of "seeds of the Gospel" through whatever good or truth could be found within this particular culture or faith.[19] Similarly, the documents challenged the members of the Church to adapt and express the gospel in ways that would be comprehensible to the surrounding culture or cultures.[20]

However, it was nearly ten years after the conclusion of the Council when Pope Paul VI specifically addressed the implementation of evangelization in his encyclical, *Evangelii Nuntiandi.* The encyclical's text builds upon several changes in the Church's understanding of evangelization or mission as described within the Vatican II documents cited above. First, the primary message of evangelization moved from an ecclesio-centric towards a Christocentric focus. Secondly, the responsibility for the propagation of the faith primarily by clergy and religious orders shifted toward a more inclusive ecclesiological approach, inviting laypersons into the missionary vocation of the Church. Finally, evangelization became positively oriented and adaptive toward the existing culture, recognizing elements consistent with the teachings of the gospel, being "capable of permeating [all cultures] without becoming subject to any one of them."[21] Thus, an inculturated evangelization would incorporate the language, signs, and symbols of those

18. Dulles, "John Paul II," 4.

19. Cf. Vatican Council II, "Lumen Gentium," 16; Vatican Council II, "Ad Gentes," 6, 9; Vatican Council II, "Gaudium et Spes," 44.

20. Here, I do not mean to suggest that the content of the gospel should be adapted; rather, the manner of how it is proclaimed or communicated should be adapted to the way in which the hearer could best receive it within the culture.

21. *EN*, 20.

being evangelized; it would attempt to answer the questions asked and have an impact on everyday life.[22]

Yet, Paul VI seems to avoid a singular definition of the term "evangelization," suggesting that:

> any partial and fragmentary definition which attempts to render the reality of evangelization in all its richness, complexity and dynamism does so only at the risk of impoverishing it and even of distorting it. It is impossible to grasp the concept of evangelization unless one tries to keep in view all its essential elements.[23]

Rather than limiting the definition of evangelization to explicit proclamation, Paul VI cites additional elements as "the renewal of humanity, witness, . . . inner adherence, entry into the community, acceptance of signs, apostolic initiative . . . "; later in this same document, he adds the necessity for ecumenical dialogue in evangelization. He recognizes that these elements may appear to be contradictory and even mutually exclusive and yet stresses that they are complementary and mutually enriching, each to be viewed in relationship with the others.[24]

Notably, pre-evangelization is first mentioned and subsequently defined in this document by Paul VI as "a first proclamation of Jesus Christ by a complex and diversified activity . . . but which is already evangelization in a true sense, although at its initial and still incomplete stage." It too, according to the pope, includes a variety of elements and "an almost indefinite range of means can be used for this purpose: explicit preaching, of course, but also art, the scientific approach, philosophical research and legitimate recourse to the sentiments of the human heart."[25] While this statement generously incorporates many hypothetical methods for pre-evangelization, Snijders criticizes the definition because, by equating pre-evangelization with evangelization *per se*, "the pope had broadened the terms to a point where they meant next to nothing."[26]

In light of documents directed specifically toward catechetics, *Catechesis Tradendae* affirms that evangelization is structured in stages or "essential moments," yet John Paul II likewise acknowledges the difficulty in

22. *EN*, 63.

23. *EN*, 17.

24. *EN*, 24.

25. *EN*, 51.

26. Snijders, "Evangelii Nuntiandi," 62.

defining the boundaries.[27] However, citing *Ad Gentes,* the *General Directory for Catechesis* claims that the stages begin with Christian witness, proceed with dialogue and presence in charity, continue with the proclamation of the gospel with a call to personal conversion, and only thereafter move into a formal catechumenate and RCIA process. From the perspective of the convert, the "moments" include an interest in the gospel, a period of searching which may be followed by an initial conversion or "act of faith" as a formal and public profession of faith, and a continuing journey of spiritual growth within the parish community.[28]

Fifteen years later, in *Redemptoris Missio,* John Paul II expanded the definition of evangelization to broadly include the proclamation of the gospel to non-Christian nations (*ad gentes*), pastoral care to existing Christian communities, and the New Evangelization. He described this third segment as "entire groups of the baptized [who] have lost a living sense of the faith, or even no longer consider themselves members of the Church, and live a life far removed from Christ and his Gospel."[29]

The process of conversion, which arguably could begin with the pre-evangelization stage, is described by the *Catechism of the Catholic Church* as an interaction or interplay between the prevenient grace of God and the individual's free acceptance of or cooperation with that grace. God initiates this process to "precede, prepare, and elicit" the human response.[30]

Since these documents were promulgated, there have been few formal definitions of pre-evangelization by the magisterium to guide the members of the Church. Perhaps it is the vagueness, or "terminological confusion," of the distinction between pre-evangelization, evangelization, and catechesis which has deferred more in-depth discussion of its meaning and implementation.[31] Another rationale for the Church not providing greater clarity may have been to allow the particular churches to adapt the methods and message according to their own cultural landscape.

---

27. John Paul II, *Catechesi Tradendae,* 18; Congregation for the Clergy, *General Directory for Catechesis,* 59, 62.

28. Congregation for the Clergy, *General Directory for Catechesis,* 47, 56.

29. *RM,* 33.

30. *CCC,* n. 2001–2, 2022. Grace may be defined as unmerited, gratuitous assistance, mercy, or benevolence from the divine toward creation.

31. E.g., Nebreda, *Kerygma,* 42. Nebreda states that even the term "catechesis" is used in "a wider sense to refer to 'any transmission of the word of God' and in a narrower sense that distinguishes it from the *kerygma* which it develops and explains."

Pre-Evangelization and Pope Francis

While the current pope, Francis, has not explicitly used the term "pre-evangelization" during his papacy, his prepapal writing suggests an awareness of the need for some type of preparation. Writing as Jorge Bergoglio, he contends that the primary issue is not the ontological but the experiential; in other words, contemporary young adults may less deny the existence of or knowledge about God, but they lack the ability to find God within themselves. He states that it is "useless" to talk about God to someone who does not know how to wrestle with or who has dismissed existential questions which, he insists, are common to human nature; for them, he insists, talk about God becomes "abstract or esoteric or a push towards a devotion that has no effect on their lives."[32] Therefore, he suggests a first step is to make sense of the buried or hidden or dying questions, but that nonetheless exist within the human person.

Perhaps a better expression of Francis' interpretation of pre-evangelization would be to observe his behavior during public interactions with nonbelieving young adults. Rather than remaining insulated among the cadre of the curia or theologians, Francis has chosen to move beyond the ecclesial boundaries (or the *ad extra*) to engage with those on the peripheries, even seeking out those who are considered on the societal fringes.

Not surprisingly, Francis' popularity extends to those without religious affiliation. A 2017 Pew Research study indicates over two-thirds (71 percent) of American religious "nones" have a "very" or "mostly" favorable view of the pope.[33] According to Barna, nearly half (49 percent) of American young adults agree that the Pope has positively influenced their view of the Catholic Church, and 34 percent say Francis has caused them to make changes to their spiritual life.[34]

A further demonstration of Francis' attentiveness to the issues of young people was the general assembly of the Synod of Bishops held in Rome in October 2018. This synod focused on young adults and the faith and included invitations for young adult representatives between 16–29. The pope provided an extensive response to this synod with his apostolic

---

32. Bergoglio, "For Man," 80, 82.
33. Gecewicz, "US Catholics."
34. Barna Group, "What Americans Think."

exhortation *Christus Vivit*, which also indicates Francis' genuine concern for the questions and concerns raised by young adults.[35]

Ever mindful of how young adults communicate and interrelate through social media, Pope Francis is not afraid to embrace and harness the power of the digital sphere for the purpose of engaging this demographic. For example, the pope regularly poses for selfies with young people, sends short messages or tweets using Twitter (with username @Pontifex) on current issues, and posts photos and messages on Instagram.[36] A recent development in the Vatican's media toolbox is the Click to Pray app, which enables young adults to pray along with the Pope on their smartphones. Through these methods, the pope becomes accessible, relatable, and authentic to young adults, which may prompt a greater receptivity to his messages. Francis' use of social media may better serve to challenge young adults to consider his words on controversial subjects and even to begin a dialogue with the beliefs of the Catholic Church.

In addition, Francis uses language that is less philosophical or theological compared to some of his predecessors; rather, it is informal, idiomatic, and frequently humorous, a style which reflects an ease with and knowledge of his audience. At the same time, he connects what appear to be purely secular interests and concerns with the values and teachings of the Catholic Church. As an example, his tweets and public statements on homosexuality, immigration, and climate change, while not deviating from Catholic teaching, may resonate with the values of contemporary young adults who have the greatest propensity to support what are considered liberal social concerns.[37] In such a way, he addresses their concerns and even introduces the teachings of Catholic Christianity without explicitly preaching the gospel message.

Like his two predecessors, Francis has frequently used the term "encounter" in reference to evangelization. Specifically, an encounter is an invitation to personally meet Jesus Christ. But the encounter does not end there, like a one-stop salvation shop. Rather, the encounter is followed by the discovery of who this Jesus, which spurs a deepening of this relationship

---

35. Francis I, *Christus Vivit*.

36. While figures vary, reportedly the Pope had between 40 million followers on Twitter and 5.1 million followers on Instagram as of the end of December 2017. There are also pope emojis or small graphic images of th pope that are frequently used in text messaging by young adults.

37. For an overview of current statistics on political and social views of American young adults, see Pew Research Center, "Millennials in Adulthood."

and desire to remain connected to him. I will unpack the language and locus of the encounter in chapter 5.

5

Pre-Evangelization as "Encounter"

OVER THE PAST TWENTY-FIVE years, papal teaching has linked the language of the phenomenon of a personal encounter with Jesus as a critical component of evangelization. For John Paul II, this encounter is the starting point of evangelization while Benedict XVI claims that evangelization is dependent upon it.[1] Why is the encounter so critical? As I discussed in chapter 2, many young adults are seeking meaning or something beyond them. However, they may not know how to satisfy this existential hunger, or it may be waiting to be awakened. Facilitating an encounter with the transcendent may be the very opening needed for young adults to hear the gospel message.

In this chapter, I will briefly explore various understandings of the term "encounter" from Scripture and the perspectives of Martin Buber, Romano Guardini, Luigi Guissani, and Popes Benedict XVI and Francis. While the *Catechism of the Catholic Church* traditionally associates the "encounter" with Christ with elements related to the liturgical practice of the Church, I believe that a wider understanding and promotion of the encounter needs to be expanded beyond the parish walls to reach unchurched young adults.

What Is an "Encounter"?

In contrast to the word "meeting," which I believe suggests an actively planned or intentional assembling of individuals, the word "encounter" implies more of an unplanned, perhaps even unexpected or perceived random

1. John Paul II, *Ecclesia in America*, 3; Benedict XVI, "Address to the Members."

connection of an individual with another. It may even include a personal intersection with an experience or event. For example, I may encounter a former classmate in a grocery store during a trip to Los Angeles or I may encounter a breathtaking sunset while driving home on the highway.

Scripturally, the concept of encounter may be grounded in descriptions of physical meetings of Jesus with the Samaritan woman at the well, the tax collector Zacchaeus, Jesus' disciples on their walk to Emmaus, and the apostle Paul (John 4:4–26; Luke 19:1–10; Luke 24:13–35; Acts 9:3–9). In each case, Jesus actively seeks out the individual and reveals his identity either gradually or suddenly, depending on the recipient's capacity to receive the revelation. In some situations, he uses a method of questioning which prompts the listener to go deeper into questioning his or her own understanding of who he is. The encounter appears to ignite a chain reaction within the one who is found. This first occurs on the subjective level, but then becomes a force which spreads outward to others. For example, the Samaritan woman rushes to tell others in her village about a possible Messiah (John 4:28–29, 39).

Martin Buber's concept and language of encounter (*Begegnung*) is situated within the structure of relationship, in the sense of the individual or subject "I" (*ich*) meeting the "Thou" (*Du*).[2] For Buber, God (who also could be perceived as the transcendent, but also as Other in contrast to the subject) is the eternal Thou who initiates the possibility of the "I-Thou" relation through grace.[3] While the individual is the recipient of the encounter, Buber believes the individual controls how the relationship will proceed based upon how the Other is perceived and addressed. To illustrate, Buber contrasts the relational difference using the language of "I-Thou" versus the "I-It." Rather than relating to the Other as Thou (*Du*), or as an equal subject as he or she truly is, Buber argues that the individual may view the Other as an object (an "it") in a disinterested, utilitarian fashion. The individual may come to know the Other as Thou, or as a subject, only by being authentically present toward the Other in his or her own true self, without seeking to see the Other through one's own lens or desires.

---

2. Buber, *Ich und Du*, 3. While the English "you" is used as an address for both individual and plural persons, as well as for both formal and informal relationships, the German *Du* is specifically spoken to an individual with which the I (*ich*) has an intimate, even familial relationship. Hence, Buber's encounter implies a closeness, an ease, even "familial" connection between one and the Other (whether as God or another person).

3. Buber, *Ich und Du*, 10.

Here, there may be congruence with Thomas Aquinas' descriptions of types of faith, e.g., the difference between *credere Deo, credere Deum*, and *credere in Deum*.[4] An individual can relate to God as an "It" by reducing their perception of God's being or self to a set formula of objective explanations. The individual may deliberately (or perhaps unconsciously) choose to perceive God as a remote or distanced deity rather than to explore knowing God on a new level through prayer. Finally, the individual may know about and be comfortable with a God on an intellectual level; he or she may even trust in a so-called Higher Power in a deistic manner, but not be able to stake one's complete faith in God as a Person, who could credibly make demands on another as a good friendship obliges. Wodehouse claims that one has "never found God, recognized and greeted and worshiped Him, until we have said Thou."[5]

Guardini likewise believes that God must initiate the encounter, however he posits that God normally does so by an external revelation rather than through "an interior movement."[6] Benedict XVI seems to pick up Guardini's theme when he proposes that an encounter contains an initial call or invitation as an intense and decisive moment requiring a response from the one encountered. Reflecting upon the example of the apostle Paul in Acts 9:1–19, Benedict suggests that Paul is changed from an "event," defined as a personal meeting with One (in this case, Christ) who the apostle had not personally sought:

> Paul never once interprets this moment as an event of conversion. Why? There are many hypotheses, but for me the reason is very clear. This turning point in his life, this transformation of his whole being was not the fruit of a psychological process, of a maturation or intellectual and moral development. Rather it came from the outside: it was not the fruit of his thought but of his encounter with Jesus Christ ... There is no other way in which to explain this renewal of Paul. None of the psychological analyses can clarify or solve the problem. This event alone, this powerful encounter with Christ, is the key to understanding what had happened.[7]

---

4. Aquinas, *Summa Theologica*, II–II.2.2; Aquinas makes a distinction between *credo Deum* ("I believe in God" with God as the object), *credo Deo* ("I believe God"), and *credere in Deum* ("I believe unto God" which includes the free assent of the will or act of faith.)

5. Wodehouse, "Martin Buber's I and Thou," 29.

6. Guardini and Kuehn, *Essential Guardini*, 62.

7. Benedict XVI, "General Audience."

Moreover, for Benedict, this renewal or becoming a Christian means experiencing such an event as "encounter" rather than simply adopting a new moral code or a philosophy.[8] Guardini goes further, explaining that the encounter not only opens the opportunity for the individual's incorporation into the "new I-Thou relationship . . . [but the individual] is enabled for the first time to rise to the stature which God intended"; in other words, the individual begins to understand his origin and destiny in light of this new relationship.[9]

Francis views the attractiveness of the encounter to be one of the most powerful incentives for growth within the Church.[10] He invites the individual to be open toward these promptings of grace and experiences of beauty. Even an initial, rudimentary communication with God may then grow in terms of personal depth and amount of information, so that the person becomes more open and comfortable in speaking to the Other as in a person-to-person relationship.

Encounter Ad Intra

The *Catechism of the Catholic Church* connects the human encounter with Jesus via other humans as well as physical objects; these are explicitly defined as the sacraments (with particular emphasis on the Eucharist), the priest, prayer, the poor, and Scripture.[11] However, many of these points of contact presume that the potential convert is already actively practicing the faith as defined by the Catholic Church. Therefore, the encounter is primarily directed toward those in the parish environment (*ad intra*).

For example, in relation to the Church's seven sacraments, baptism is considered the normative introductory sacrament in which a child or adult is initiated into the life of the Church; the act is likened to both Jesus' own baptism in the Gospels of Matthew and John and described by Paul as a kind of participation in Jesus' own death and resurrection.[12] An unbaptized person cannot be a valid recipient of the other sacraments until he or she has been baptized.[13] Even in the case of "sacramentalized Catholics," including those

8. Benedict XVI, "General Audience."

9. Guardini and Kuehn, *Essential Guardini*, 62–64.

10. E.g., *EG*, 15, 142, 167.

11. *CCC*, n. 1373.

12. *CCC*, n. 1212–28.

13. *CIC*, col. 842.

baptized and even those who participate in Mass, some are not even sure that one can have a personal encounter with Jesus.[14]

Secondly, in the fortunate case where a young adult has experienced a positive interaction with a priest inside or outside the physical structure of a parish, it is also likely that others may have had poor experiences with a priest. However, I am skeptical if many unchurched young adults will deliberately visit a church unprompted and hence, will never meet a priest as part of their spiritual journey until after a conscious decision is made to investigate the Catholic Church through the formal RCIA process.

Thirdly, the Catechism claims that a person can encounter Jesus through prayer. Statistics show that many young adults, even if they do not self-identify as religious, practice some form of prayer.[15] This might appear to be an encouraging avenue. However, in his interviews with Millennials, John Mabry discovered that their motivations for prayer were more congruent with Christian Smith's fourth tenet related to Moral Therapeutic Deism.[16] The god to which they prayed is viewed more as a divine genie, distantly waiting (but not too eagerly) to grant wishes. Prayer for a young adult could be identified as a religious or spiritual experience through a kind of communication with a known or unknown transcendent figure, however this experience does not need to be specifically linked with the person of Jesus or even, for that matter, to a personal God. The figure of God may be perceived in relation to the subject, not as the transcendent may truly be.

Fourthly, the Catechism claims that a person can have a spiritual experience with Christ through a physical encounter with the poor. Here, the Catechism does not distinguish the materially versus the spiritually poor. As many young adults today are drawn to humanitarian service

---

14. Weddell, *Forming Intentional Disciples*, 43–46. Weddell quotes John Paul II's statement in CT which indicates that a baptized person may only have the *capacity* to believe. Catholic theology, based upon the writings of Thomas Aquinas (Aquinas, *Summa Theologiae*, III, 69.10), teaches that any graces received by a sacrament may be "in potential," requiring the human to actively respond to the grace with a sincere act, thereby activating the effects of the grace.

15. According to Pew Research Center, "America's Changing Religious Landscape," 46 percent of Older Millennials (born 1981–89) and 39 percent of Younger Millennials (born 1990–96) responded that they pray daily. This contrasts with 56 percent of Gen X.

16. Mabry, *Faithful Generations*, 172–75, 177–80. Smith's fourth tenet is "God does not need to be particularly involved in one's life except when God is needed to resolve a problem."

projects, it is quite possible that some may intuit or sense a presence of Christ at this basic level.[17]

Finally, the Catechism declares that the Christian Scriptures, both Old and New Testaments, are means of encountering Jesus. Theologically, many Christian faith traditions associate the written scriptures as the "word of God" with the person of Jesus Christ as the Word of God. Yet, the Barna Group found that 62 percent of polled non-Christian Millennials claimed they never read the Bible; an additional 15 percent indicated they had read the Bible less than once a year. Moreover, within this same group, 71 percent indicated that they had no desire to read the Bible more.[18]

If young adults are not encountering God or Jesus Christ through the traditional or conventional avenues provided by the Catholic Church, then I suggest that some form of encounter will need to take place outside of the physical confines of the parish building.

Encounter Ad Extra

As with any of the previously cited examples, an encounter with the transcendent (whether consciously identified as God or Jesus Christ) could spontaneously occur outside the parish setting without the active seeking of the participant. However, to a nonbeliever, experiencing an actual and real encounter with a physical, historical figure might appear to be illogical and impossible. Mercadante's research shows that "nones" question the existence of "a sovereign, transcendent, and personal deity." Smith's 2009 research found that even young adult Catholics scored the lowest among all Christian denominations with 62 percent claiming that God is "a personal being in the lives of people today."[19]

However, the essence of the Catholic principle of sacramentality holds that all of creation can be a conduit for or lead one to the divine. Hence, McBrien asserts that the encounter with God is through a mediated human experience or through a sensible object.[20] While Buber does not believe that

---

17. According to Pew Research Center, "beyond marriage and family, 21 percent of Millennials say that helping people who are in need is one of the most important things in their life" (Pew Research Center, "Millennials: A Portrait," 18). "Nearly six-in-ten (57 percent) Millennials say that they had volunteered in the past 12 months" (ibid., 83).

18. Barna Group, "Millennials and the Bible."

19. Mercadante, "Seeker Next Door," 32; Smith and Snell, *Souls in Transition*, 119.

20. McBrien, *Catholicism*, 11.

there can be a created intermediary between the individual and God,[21] he does argue that "all actual life is encounter."[22] Thus, he admits the possibility of every experience in creation to act as a conduit of the presence of God. Likewise, Guissani proposes that every part of "life is a web of events and encounters" and the individual's reactions to these.[23]

Specifically, Buber believes that God, as the Eternal Thou, can be present and perhaps even discernable in every ordinary "other" whom the individual may encounter in the course of a day. Guissani adds that, since Christ is no longer historically present, anyone can "become an encounter for companions and friends," implying a kind of mysterious presence of Christ within his followers.[24]

However, each of these encounters or events does not necessarily lead to a connection to God. Guissani argues that the encounter must present something that is new, true, fresh, and of value to the individual. One must be "provoked or helped by something different from ourselves, by something objective, by something that we 'encounter.'"[25] Thus, the event needs to be independent of the individual and, at the same time, the individual must have the capacity to perceive meaning within the encounter, together with an awareness of the connection between his subjective being and this meaning.

In addition, Buber suggests that the individual must first cultivate the Thou relationship in the other human being before one can come to know God as Thou. When two or more individuals are fully present to each other, each accepting the other as subject rather than object, he suggests one can experience God as Thou through the space between or among them.[26] Ultimately, Guardini suggests that each of these events calls the individual to

---

21. Buber believes that God is not a remote entity to be merely "believed in," with whom we cannot communicate, but rather is one with whom human beings may "live with" in a kind of relationship; true communication is not only possible but necessary with this God. Just as continual dialogue between the "I" and the "Thou" grows and sustains the human relationship, Buber believes we encounter God through dialogue. We can speak; he can be listened to.

22. Buber, *Ich und Du*, 62.

23. Guissani, *Religious Sense*, 36.

24. Guissani, *Journey to Truth*, 95.

25. Guissani, *Journey to Truth*, 105.

26. Buber, *Ich und Du*, 75–83.

some form of surrender, whether to a person, idea, or task, which facilitates the movement toward the encounter with and surrender to God.[27]

Pope Francis, however, insists that the "I-Thou" encounter between person-to-God must be extended to the wider community of faith, which is the Church. The fruit of the encounter cannot remain at the individual decision or private relationship between the person and God.[28] Moreover, Francis challenges the Church to a "culture of encounter." I interpret this phrase to mean that Christians must go outside of their comfort zones, allowing themselves to meet the other (who may be radically different than the individual) and be met by him or her, to be open to his or her individuality, value, and dignity as made in the image and likeness of God.[29]

In other words, pre-evangelization cannot be approached passively. The call to encounter will challenge the Christian to move actively and outwardly from the parish. At this juncture, however, I am not advocating that the nonbeliever is ready to become incorporated into the wider body of the Church; indeed, this invitation may be premature and preemptive. Rather, I would propose that within the RCIA (Rite of Christian Initiation of Adults) process, the nonbeliever can be slowly introduced to the community through small groups which meet regularly in the period of the catechumenate.

Perhaps one of the most attractive features about the concept of encounter as a method of pre-evangelization is that it may reduce the tendency of narrowly evaluating the experience in terms of results alone. Giussani encourages believers that "since we haven't arranged the encounter, our actions are not conditioned by our success."[30] In other words, sometimes those who evangelize (e.g., in the strictest meaning of evangelization as the explicit verbal proclamation of the gospel) may tend to become discouraged when they do not see immediate fruits of their labor.[31] Since the encounter is less

27. Guardini and Kuehn, *Essential Guardini,* 62.

28. Francis I, *Lumen Fidei,* 39.

29. John Allen, in "Francis and the 'Culture of Encounter,'" notes that the phrase "culture of encounter" is "elastic enough to embrace a wide range of possible meanings, but in general Francis seems to intend the idea of reaching out, fostering dialogue and friendship even outside the usual circles, and making a special point of encountering people who are neglected and ignored by the wider world."

30. Giussani, *Journey to Truth,* 95.

31. John Paul II states, "Internal and external difficulties must not make us pessimistic or inactive. What counts, here as in every area of Christian life, is the confidence that comes from faith, from the certainty that it is not we who are the principal agents of the Church's mission, but Jesus Christ and his Spirit. We are only coworkers . . ." (*RM,* 36).

of a predetermined meeting, allowing God to arrange the circumstances, the witness simply needs to be present to the daily events of life and to the Other as he or she is at the moment. Even if the nonbeliever shows no external signs of further interest, Giussani claims that a stimulating person-to-person encounter can remain as a positive memory for individuals who do not close themselves off through their own preconceptions.[32]

If evangelization is about encountering Christ as a person, then the initial encounter in pre-evangelization is both an opportunity and invitation to discover and nurture the desire to do so. But can there be obstacles in responding to pre-evangelistic encounters? Do preconceptions of religion, Christianity, or Jesus prevent the unchurched from moving on to a stage of wanting to learn or know Christ? Many Protestant denominations tend to associate pre-evangelization with overcoming intellectual roadblocks. In the next chapter, I will look at examples of pre-evangelization from the perspective of our Protestant brothers and sisters.

32. Giussani, *Journey to Truth*, 95.

6

Protestant Views of Pre-Evangelization

THE CATHOLIC CHURCH IS not alone in its advocacy and use of pre-evangelization in the conversion process. In this chapter, I will provide a brief survey of views and practices of pre-evangelization by Protestant denominations. American Protestant theologians and clergy tend to use the term "pre-evangelism" rather than "pre-evangelization." I suggest that the two terms have similar connotations and will use the terms "pre-evangelization" and "pre-evangelism" interchangeably in this chapter.

William Abraham asserts that the roots of these terms—"evangelization" and "evangelism"—emerged only in the late nineteenth century with virtually no difference in meaning; however, he surmises that the term "evangelization" is perhaps considered a bit less pejorative. He explains that the Reformers sought to limit the term to proclamation but that the Protestant connotation eventually included the establishment of new church communities.[1] But while the term "evangelism" is relatively ubiquitous and its practice encouraged among many Protestant faith communities, my research indicated that usage of the term and praxis of "pre-evangelism" is not.

To illustrate, not all Protestant confessional bodies employ this term and still others do not acknowledge the concept. For example, Karl Barth and his followers were reluctant to recognize or espouse the need for pre-evangelism out of their conviction that God must be the absolute agent of

---

1. Abraham, *Logic of Evangelism*, 40, 92.

conversion.[2] While the Christian believer acts as a witness to God's revelation in obedience to God's command, this role is paradoxically superfluous.[3] Rather, the person is utterly dependent upon God to reveal truth through the Word of God, expressed through Scripture.[4] Some Protestants view the use of pre-evangelism as a substitute for evading or avoiding the explicit proclamation of the gospel. McManis claims there is nothing explicitly taught in Scripture by Jesus or his apostles to justify the concept or practice of pre-evangelism.[5] Some Protestants may have been reluctant to embrace the term and its implications because it would diminish or threaten the inherent power of the gospel message to bring about an instantaneous conversion. Therefore, the need for pre-evangelism might suggest that conversion is more multi-dimensional and process-oriented. Such lack of enthusiasm to embrace pre-evangelism may also have resulted from a revivalist paradigm of conversion which dominated American Protestant history in the eighteenth and nineteenth centuries.

Arguably, by the early 1900s, Presbyterian J. Gresham Machen may have been one of the first Protestant theologians to acknowledge the critical need for pre-evangelism without explicitly using the term. Machen acknowledges the primacy of God's grace which influences the nonbeliever; however, he also notes a cooperative role of the evangelizer.[6] Admitting the

2. Barth, "Doctrine of Reconciliation," 535. Barth claims that "there can be no preparation" for the grace God extends through the command of Christ to the elect. Therefore, I would say he sees man's response as more an act of obedience (ibid., 538). Further, in Barth's "Awakening to Conversion" (Section 4), 553–84, God appears to give a "jolt" or "shock" to the sleeping human, sometimes using creaturely or natural things moved by the divine. But the awakening is "not the work of one of the creaturely factors, coefficients or agencies which are there at work and can be seen, but of the will and act of God who uses these factors and Himself makes them coefficients and agencies for this purpose, setting them in motion as such in the meaning and direction in which He has appointed." There is a "coordination between the two elements [i.e., wholly creaturely and wholly divine] but absolute primacy of the divine over the creaturely" (ibid., 557).

3. "When a man is a witness to another, he can only tell him about something, and answer for the truth and reality of what is told. None of us can reveal to the other than God loves him and that he may love God in return" (Barth, "Doctrine of Reconciliation," 815).

4. Greer, *Mapping Postmodernism*, 102.

5. McManis, *Biblical Apologetics*, 32.

6. Machen, "Christianity and Culture," 7. At the same time, he realizes that an intellectual argument by itself is not enough to effect conversion. He notes that the "inward experience" and "change of heart" that are essential to conversion can only be produced by the "power of God" (ibid., 5, 11).

affective and experiential components of conversion, he suggests that the primary obstacles exist on the intellectual level.[7] As Machen states:

> It would be a great mistake to suppose that all men [sic] are equally well prepared to receive the gospel. It is true that the decisive thing is the regenerative power of God. That can overcome all lack of preparation, and the absence of that makes even the best preparation useless. But as a matter of fact God usually exerts that power in connection with certain prior conditions of the human mind, and it should be ours to create, so far as we can, with the help of God, those favorable conditions for the reception of the gospel. False ideas are the greatest obstacles to the reception of the gospel. We may preach with all the fervor of a reformer and yet succeed only in winning a straggler here and there, if we permit the whole collective thought of the nation or of the world to be controlled by ideas which, by the resistless force of logic, prevent Christianity from being regarded as anything more than a harmless delusion. Under such circumstances, what God desires us to do is to destroy the obstacle at its root.[8]

Nebreda proposed that some Protestant theologians, as early as the mid-1960s, began to question a purely kerygmatic approach, which had been the *de facto* practice of evangelism for nearly a half century.[9] Theologians began to point to the example of Paul's address to the Greek Gentiles on Mars Hill as a model for engaging a non-Christian culture using extra-biblical proofs such as natural theology, Epicurean and Stoic poetry, philosophy, and reason (Acts 17:22–31).

Several Protestant theologians who support the use of pre-evangelism share some level of consensus in their affirmation of the critical component of preparation. Anglican Alistair McGrath claims that "apologetics [as pre-evangelism] lays the ground" for the invitation or call to conversion, while explicit evangelism "extends it."[10] Methodist theologians Norman and David Geisler, who are father and son, write that pre-evangelism "tills the ground, prepares the soil to receive the seed," a reference to Jesus' parable in the Synoptic Gospels (cf. Matt 3:13–23; Mark 4:3–20; Luke 8:5–15). Van Dop does not use the term "pre-evangelism" in his dissertation, but he coins a term "peri-conversion" (meaning "around conversion") to distinguish

7. Machen, "Christianity and Culture," 7, 11.

8. Machen, "Christianity and Culture," 7.

9. Nebreda, *Kerygma*, 47.

10. McGrath, *Mere Apologetics*, 22–23.

conversion as a singular, bounded event from a process or development, which may include pre-evangelization.[11]

One of the most recognizable methods within Protestant pre-evangelism is the use of apologetics. The term "apologetics" comes from the Greek word *apologia*, meaning a kind of speech of defense. Therefore, apologetics can be defined as both an offensive and defensive argument for the truth of Christianity, sometimes in a polemical context. This approach tends to focus on the intellectual faculties, rather than the affective behavior, of the nonbeliever. For example, Presbyterian R. C. Sproul specifically mentions that pre-evangelism should include any data or information which must be processed by the individual before he can accept or reject the gospel.[12]

Steven Cowan separates apologetics into five categories. Classical apologetics relies on natural theology to prove a theistic worldview, meaning that one accepts the existence of God who continues to act within creation. Historical (sometimes also known as evidential) apologetics stresses the validity of certain historical experiences or evidence of miracles to prove Christianity. Cumulative-case apologetics utilizes both classical and historical/evidential methods to build a case for Christianity, which may be comparable to how a lawyer develops an argument but in a less formalized manner. The presuppositional method attempts to demonstrate to nonbelievers that their worldview cannot explain the inconsistencies between their experience and reality.[13] The fifth category posited by Cowan, Reformed epistemology, I would argue is wrongly identified as a kind of apologetics as it considers that one does not necessarily need a rational proof to accept the premise of Christianity on faith.[14]

Apologetics, used in a pre-evangelistic manner, does not necessarily include a listing of proofs for Christianity. Evangelical Randy Newman describes pre-evangelism as "leveling the playing field" in relation to dialogue between Christians and nonbelievers.[15] He suggests that nonbelievers' preconceived understanding and prejudices against the Christian faith

11. Van Dop, "Connecting to God," 100, 180.

12. Sproul, *Defending Your Faith*, 23.

13. Two approaches fall under this category: (1) the rational, empirical, and deductive promoted by Cornelius Van Til, and (2) the inductive espoused by Francis Schaeffer. However, I would argue that Schaeffer is also relational, as his L'Abri method engages and addresses the individual not merely on the intellectual side but also on the affective and communal.

14. Cowan, *Five Views*, 15–20.

15. Newman, "Leveling the Playing Field," 1.

can be overcome by questioning and challenging their allegations.[16] In his book, *Questioning Evangelism: Engaging People's Hearts the Way Jesus Did*, Newman calls this method "rabbinic questioning" where one attempts to respond to a question with another question with the goal of helping the nonbeliever see both sides of the issue, particularly as related to faith.[17] The choice of nonbelief can be as much a "faith statement" without a logical foundation. This is a similar argument as Nebreda's rationale for pre-evangelization, described earlier in this chapter. However, Kinnaman and Lyons suggest that, because young adults process information nonlinearly, they are unlikely to change their beliefs because of evidence produced by slick arguments or apologetics.[18]

Sometimes the use of apologetics is accompanied by a space for the nonbeliever to ask questions. Evangelical Francis Schaeffer who, with his wife, founded the L'Abri Fellowship (which attracted many young adults) in Switzerland during the late 1950s, believed that the United States since the mid-1900s had become increasingly hostile toward Christianity. Because of this change in receptivity, he stressed that initial arguments on behalf of Christianity would be next to impossible. A purely kerygmatic evangelism had failed because Christians "had not taken the time with pre-evangelism."[19]

Schaeffer observed that all humans hold presuppositions, which are beliefs or theories often absorbed by the tribe or prevailing culture and unconsciously accepted; these often consciously or unconsciously affect the way a person subsequently makes decisions and values.[20] Influenced by Hegel's dialectic and echoing Machen, Schaeffer proposes that the Christian's role is to uncover these presuppositions (Schaeffer's term is "removing the roof") to help the nonbeliever understand how his or her own worldview is illogical, inconsistent, and in tension with the "real world."[21] By "real world," Schaeffer means the external world and its form and the nature of humanity.[22]

16. Newman, "Leveling the Playing Field," 2.

17. Newman, *Questioning Evangelism*.

18. Kinnaman and Lyons, *unChristian*, 70.

19. Schaeffer, *Complete Works*, 155.

20. According to Schaeffer, *Complete Works*, 326: "Most people do get their presuppositions from their family and from society, without knowing it."

21. Schaeffer, *Complete Works*, 131–34, 140. Schaeffer uses both terms "roof" and "shelter" to indicate a kind of system of protection that seems to shield the individual from the reality of nature.

22. Throughout his writings, Schaeffer describes this anthropology as "mannishness"; I suggest that he intends to mean "nature."

Perhaps the foundational and central aspect of Schaeffer's apologetics was his love for the individual, which was strongly grounded in his belief that each person is made in the image of God and hence, should be treated with dignity.[23] It is out of this conviction, Schaeffer insists, that the environment in which the nonbeliever relates and interacts becomes a critical element. The L'Abri experience sought to provide its visitors with a strong sense of hospitality together with an openness and space to ask questions. Schaeffer fostered the importance of first listening with the intention to "learn the questions of the generation" before speaking.[24] While intellectual engagement and respectful dialogue was strongly encouraged, the inquirer was not to be coerced into making a premature religious commitment.

Norman and Dave Geisler's method of pre-evangelism centers around relationship-building through conversation. Their approach seems to be more structured or intentional toward the goal of personal conversion. For example, conversations are categorized as hearing, illuminating, uncovering, and building.[25] In each stage, the evangelizer is encouraged to identify fallacies in a person's set of beliefs, ask probing questions to stimulate uncertainty and reveal barriers to the gospel, and finally to "correct" the person through a type of apologetics. Facts about Jesus (which are defined as "objective evidence") and reasons for belief are then connected to the individual's perception of the practice of the Christian faith (defined as "subjective experience"). Using Cowan's definitions outlined earlier, this style could be considered "cumulative case" apologetics, involving aspects of both presuppositional and classical.

While the Geislers' method has merit in terms of its structure and ease in guiding evangelizers in their efforts, I would criticize it as a reductionist approach based upon rehearsed questions and answers. Francois Trembley, an atheist blogger, finds this method "manipulating."[26] Teasdale claims the Geisler method is contrived and questions whether the evangelizer cares about the friendship or relationship itself or is primarily concerned about moving the conversation toward the ultimate goal of conversion; further, he claims that the suggested method is geared toward memorization of stock answers than a genuine dialogue.[27]

23. Schaeffer, *Complete Works*, 131, 176.
24. Schaeffer, *Complete Works*, 414.
25. Geisler and Geisler, *Conversational Evangelism*.
26. Tremblay, "Geisler's Evangelistic Questions."
27. Teasdale, "Review of *Conversational Evangelism*," 29.

Evangelical Donald Bloesch views pre-evangelism as either "functional apologetics" or "Good Samaritan service." He affirms the importance of meeting nonbelievers where they are and using understandable language. He encourages friendship and charity as a means of pre-evangelism as opposed to "philosophical preparation."[28] This style can be illustrated by both Jesus' example of healing the sick and feeding the hungry in Scripture and the approach of William Booth's Salvation Army. Booth felt people would be more open to receiving the gospel after they had personally experienced care and love by others.[29] The inclusion of humanitarian service as pre-evangelism sets Bloesch's method apart from the other Protestant theologians highlighted above.

From the sources reviewed above, the Protestant application of pre-evangelism appears to have evolved from exclusively or primarily addressing the cognitive elements related to conversion. However, I would suggest that pre-evangelism seems to retain a polemical or argumentative inclination by attempting to convince nonbelievers about the "wrongness" of their beliefs or reversing the worldviews of nonbelievers. There is a noticeable anthropocentric shift in recent decades in recognition of the relationship between social and physical factors and the potentiality for receptivity toward the gospel message.

After reviewing both Catholic and Protestant interpretations of pre-evangelization, can a model be offered which helps pastoral leaders and laypeople "do" pre-evangelization? In the next chapter, I will propose such a model for faith formation which addresses the contemporary mindset of young adults.

---

28. Bloesch, *Theological Notebook*, 291.
29. Bloesch, *Theology of Word and Spirit*, 240.

7

The Hermeneutical-Communicative Model and Pre-Evangelization

WHEN I ORIGINALLY BEGAN my research into the topic of pre-evangelization, I confess that I naively thought there was a single existing model for reaching American young adult "nones." While I no longer espouse this belief, I do think that a model can be helpful as a lens through which various methods of pre-evangelization can be evaluated. In this chapter, I will introduce the Hermeneutical-Communicative Model (HCM) as a model for faith formation. Understanding the development of previous catechetical theories and praxis can help distinguish this model's didactical style, the role of the teacher, and the general state of the Church within the wider society. While I admit some misgivings with the HCM in relation to pre-evangelization, I believe that it addresses the religiously pluralistic culture in which contemporary American young adults interrelate.

What Is a "Model"?

The term "model" is used in a variety of academic disciplines, however, the term is used differently within these. For example, a model can be a representation of something larger or more difficult to explain. A model can highlight some features and neglect others; it can provide an arrangement of concepts that outline a vision of a phenomenon from a peculiar perspective.

Within the discipline of theology, a model can assume a unique context and represent a different theological starting point and presuppositions. Scharlemann claims that a theological model "differs from a description because the content of a model is not intended to be a replica of how an object appears or really is . . . [but] it does allow one to come to terms with the object . . . [therefore, a model is] constructed, not naturally given . . . "[1] Klemm and Klink advocate models "as tentative, exploratory means for understanding new phenomena" that can help explain why certain observables are correlated.[2] Yet an effective model must adequately explain the current reality. If a model "no longer enables a subject really to deal with the object in question, there is nothing to prevent its being replaced by a different and more adequate one."[3] Finally, in the context of practical theology, a model may serve as a theory which moves toward praxis.

Early Faith Formation Models

In order to provide a contrast of models in faith formation I would like to briefly review several examples of earlier approaches which I discussed in chapter 3. Up to the early 1960s, the praxis of catechetics was dominated by a deductive (or top-down) teaching style. This means that content flowed from a presentation of facts with an assumed application to "real life." Whether applied in a doctrinal or kerygmatic model, this deductive method functioned reasonably well at this time because the culture was fairly homogenous and Christianized. One "learned in religion" or "learned within religion" because one was already steeped in a culture of Christianity and Christian values. The teacher (at this time, most likely a priest, religious sister, or brother) served as a witness, primarily handing down the tenets of the Church to a passive audience.

After Vatican II, an inductive didactic followed which was aligned with correlation thinking.[4] An inductive approach begins with the individual as he or she is now and applies the content of revelation to that state. A correlation method or style in relation to catechetics or evangelization may be attributed to Paul Tillich, who argued that theology is a correlation of existential questions that emerge from cultural experience and the

1. Scharlemann, "Theological Models," 70.
2. Klemm and Klink, "Constructing and Testing," 507.
3. Scharlemann, "Theological Models," 70.
4. Pollefeyt, "Difference Matters," 10.

corresponding answers from the Christian message.[5] As Tillich defines it, the "questions implied in the situation [are matched] with the answers supplied in the message."[6] The General Directory of Catechesis §151 describes a similar methodology as "existential (ascending), which moves from human problems and conditions and enlightens them with the word of God." In this model, the teacher (often still a priest or religious, but increasingly a layperson) played a role of either specialist or moderator.

Those who grew up in the 1970s, predominantly Gen X, would likely be familiar with this inductive but also very experiential style, which was widely utilized in schools and parishes. Catechetics during this era emphasized less the transmission of content. Rather, students were often encouraged to design banners or collages representing their experience and connection to faith.

In the mid 1970s and throughout the following two decades, another shift occurred in light of a growing secularization of society. Rather than positioning Christianity as the only faith, the instructor began to treat religion in a neutral way as merely a kind of "school subject," while respecting that students might have doubts and varying opinions about Christianity in light of their own backgrounds and traditions. Thus, the student learned "about religion" in an almost generic sense.

By the end of the 1980s and into the 1990s, the growing plurality of religious faiths and even the greater acceptance of agnostic and atheistic options, as well as the "spiritual but not religious" choice, meant that the instructor had to be open to discussions on multiple levels. Christianity as a religion would be offered as a rule of ethics and source of meaning. The transition moved to "learning from religion." Yet students could pick and choose from many other possible options. This transition to a spiritual smorgasbord meant that students would now learn "from religion" without having to embrace the content of a faith in totality.

Dillen and Pollefeyt raise concerns about the value of a purely inductive approach, arguing that it is much too subjective without a reference point to Christianity. They likewise reject a correlation method that rigidly links life experience with the Christian tradition and assumes a logical connection between the two worldviews. Their criticism lies in both the methodology which assumes a facile leap from the individual's daily life

5. Tillich, *Dynamics of Faith*, 36.
6. Tillich, *Dynamics of Faith*, 8.

to a language of faith and the loss of relevance when the culture or society becomes less Christian.[7]

Introducing the HCM

In 2004, Herman Lombaerts and Didier Pollefeyt proposed the Hermeneutical-Communicative Model as a contemporary approach for faith formation, which was designed for implementation in Roman Catholic secondary schools in Belgium's Flanders region.[8] The term "hermeneutics" refers to a multitude of processes of interpretation in different fields.[9] For example, when considering a hermeneutic for the study of Scripture, one might look at the text itself, the context, the author and audience, as well as the historical background. The use of the term "hermeneutic" in this model assumes that the human person is a "hermeneutical being." This means that each person comes to an understanding or knowledge through their own unique lens of experience and beliefs. While one's experience can be correlated with the Christian Tradition, it does not automatically and exclusively [need] to be.[10] So, rather than presuming we all share the same belief in an objective truth according to the Christian message, the HCM assumes that there are a multiplicity of truths or beliefs. This reflects the current situation in the United States where Christian religion and beliefs, while predominant in American history, have now become only one of many available traditions in our culture.

A hermeneutical approach to faith formation (including pre-evangelization) means that we allow each person to discover their own and others' religious or ideological presuppositions. It also means that we reinforce this awareness so that individuals can engage with the wide variety of backgrounds and experiences, contexts, and traditions of the participants in the classroom. When a number of these interpretations about faith, belief, or sacred texts come together in a conversation, a "hermeneutical intersection" emerges. Suddenly, students become aware that their outlook and situation can be experienced and interpreted differently in the light of a plurality of religious and nonreligious worldviews and traditions. Hermeneutical

---

7. Dillen and Pollefeyt, "Catechesis Inside Out," 154–55.
8. Lombaerts and Pollefeyt, "Emergence of Hermeneutics," 3–53.
9. Dillen and Pollefeyt, "Catechesis Inside Out," 157.
10. Pollefeyt, "Difference Matters," 13.

intersections can occur even where there are multiple interpretations on a topic or interest, such as care for the environment.

Pollefeyt claims that, through this exchange, the individual learns to discover their own presuppositions of religion and faith as well as those of others. This allows them to deconstruct and reconstruct their own narrative, which they then own and can defend before others. According to Fowler, this exposure to new and often multiple viewpoints is what stimulates the Individuative-Reflective stage. And this is exactly where I would argue young adults should be encouraged to move in their spiritual journey.

The term "communicative" in the HCM refers to didactical processes (or the way in which we teach). This technique and process of teaching responds to situations when multiple perspectives of the participants in a group challenge one another and hence, these differences must be worked out through communication or dialogue; the technique can effectively adapt the various perspectives into material for reflection.[11] Tension among these differences may prompt a healthy dialogue or it may regress into arguments, distancing, and increased and entrenched polarity. The goal of the communicative approach is to facilitate the process of dialogue and help the person find their own truth among the multiplicity of interpretations of experience. According to the model, the two prongs of "hermeneutic" and "communicative" cannot be separated as they are equally essential.

According to Dillen and Pollefeyt, the "critical correction" to the inductive method, without completely rejecting it, is the abductive method. Abduction means a movement away from a belief that is already there. It does not introduce or impose a completely new idea (deduction) nor does it derive something completely new from something already existing (induction). Rather, abduction takes a middle ground between the faith-to-experience deductive method and the experience-to-faith inductive method. While the contemporary culture may be de-Christianized, it assumes that there are still kernels of the Christian tradition. The role of the student is therefore to become aware of these,[12] while the role of the instructor is to facilitate and uncover these in an intentional way.

In the HCM, the teacher or instructor of religious education within a classroom setting takes on three hermeneutical roles: specialist, moderator, and witness. Rather than acting as an authority figure who simply announces the position of the Church or presents their own interpretation of Scripture,

11. Pollefeyt, "Reader: Course Didactics," 17.
12. Dillen and Pollefeyt, "Catechesis Inside Out," 161.

the instructor is a specialist or an expert in the subject matter. They are able to carefully and accurately explain the details of their belief or faith to the student. While they accept their own religious identity, they also recognize, accept, and affirm that other viewpoints and beliefs exist. They become moderators in the sense of initiating and facilitating the dialogue with the individual as the student attempts to discover and formulate their own beliefs and meaning.[13] This role may also include meditating dialogue among multiple students. As a witness, the instructor becomes an ambassador for their own faith tradition, providing a personal testimony based on their own experience.

Analyzing the Models for Pre-Evangelization

Given the catechetical models described above, the Bangkok Study's call for the need for pre-evangelization fits between the timeframes associated with the transition away from the deductive toward the inductive and correlation styles. This explains why Nebreda stressed the anthropocentric roots of this preparatory phrase of evangelization. Likewise, Pollefeyt speaks of the anthropological departure point[14] in the HCM, because each person is a hermeneutical being. "One begins by taking seriously the initial situation of the students," says Pollefeyt. "Not just the individual biography of the student but the society and class as well."[15] The individual therefore starts where she or he is now and takes ownership of his or her own faith journey, in contrast to a creed which is imposed by an outside expert or authority.

While Dillen and Pollefeyt disapprove of correlation, many apologetic approaches of pre-evangelization employ this style, seeking to uncover presuppositions and fallacies of arguments against the Christian faith, thereby realigning and supporting the truth of Christian beliefs. But one of the reasons why contemporary pre-evangelization cannot employ correlation methods is simply because there is a decreased literacy of biblical and Christian concepts. Further, the lack of the metanarrative removes Christianity as the only "message" to which the questions can be correlated.

For example, if I try to connect an experience of a contemporary unchurched young adult with a story or lesson from Scripture, I will likely get a blank stare. In some cases, the young adult may have no idea of my reference

13. Pollefeyt, "Class Notes," 14.
14. Pollefeyt, "Difference Matters," 10.
15. Pollefeyt, "Difference Matters," 15.

or connotation. And though I may not have the explicit intention to do so, the individual may allege that I am trying to convert him or her, only because I have now inserted the subject of religion into the conversation.

Therefore, I agree with many of the premises outlined by Dillen and Pollefeyt in which the HCM would apply. First, the model reflects the multicultural and multi-religious world in which contemporary American young adults live, as well as the cultural rejection of objective truth.[16] A new paradigm for pre-evangelization must account for the plurality of religious and nonreligious beliefs. At the same time, it does not mean that Christianity is completely removed from the whole smorgasbord.

Second, the HCM acknowledges the existence of semi-religious elements within the American culture. Pollefeyt advocates that the teacher be equipped with the "skill to trace religious elements in the experiences that resound in the stories of pupils, and to communicatively interpret and reflect on these elements."[17] In pre-evangelization, this abductive approach may find a connection with Newman's illative sense. For example, training and strengthening in this sense can help the young adult to recognize threads of the transcendent in the ordinary and routine of daily life. This discovery can then challenge the individual to draw hypotheses and take small steps of faith despite entertaining normal doubts.

Third, the HCM seeks to address the gap between Christianity and the culture and allows for a plethora of perspectives. It also allows for a diversity of interpretations of the method by bringing in various stimulants for dialogue, including films, books, music, or art.[18] Pre-evangelization also utilizes multiple means as a conduit for an encounter with transcendence.

My greatest criticism of the HCM is that it assumes a captive audience within a school or parish environment. For example, Pollefeyt assumes a triad of object (as religion), subject (as audience, in this case the student), and institution (as school);[19] the institution includes *de facto* a communal setting of students and teacher. Given this context of student and teacher, the HCM would more strictly relate to the more formalized parish RCIA program, in particular the pre-catechumenate stage where young adults are allowed to question and explore their faith prior to making a public commitment through the Rite of Acceptance to continue formal catechesis.

16. Dillen and Pollefeyt, "Catechesis Inside Out," 159.
17. Pollefeyt, "Class Notes," 10.
18. Dillen and Pollefeyt, "Catechesis Inside Out," 58.
19. Pollefeyt, "Difference Matters," 10.

In addition, the HCM presupposes an environment in which the child or teenager is exposed to some type of formal religious education, as is common in many Western European school structures. Formal religious education also takes place in most American parish settings for children who do not attend faith-based schools. Most American students attend public schools, which do not include religious education as part of the curriculum. If the child or teen is raised within a familial structure which is either nonreligious or nonpracticing, he or she will likewise not receive formal catechesis within the parish or church. This gap, therefore, needs to be replaced with an alternative.

Adapting the HCM to Pre-Evangelization Ad Extra

How can one translate and adapt this model outside the religious school or parish to the secular environment? This is the locus, I have argued, where pre-evangelization predominantly occurs today. In contrast to an organized group setting, such as in a parish where religious education classes and RCIA programs occur, encounters *ad extra* which are associated with pre-evangelization may more likely occur on an individual rather than a communal basis. Within this encounter, the believer should be willing and able to initiate and sustain conversation with a nonbeliever or even someone who self-identifies as "spiritual but not religious." This is the essential "communicative" component of where the HCM really fits pre-evangelization. If necessary, the believer can help the other become aware of Christian thought and ideals already in their background experience and culture. The believer can probe into what the other thinks, which prompts the other to articulate or at least begin to consider exactly what they believe.

In situations where the conversation includes many individuals (and hence, the possibility of a variety of viewpoints), the believer may also be responsible for moderating and mediating dialogue among multiple individuals. The initial phase in this conversation, according to Pollefeyt, is known as "unpacking."[20] The believer might carefully listen and be attentive to presuppositions, filtering erroneous statements, and affirming where there is ambiguity. The believer might consider: What is the lens through which the other views faith, religion, and Catholic Christianity in particular? Are there particular experiences which have contributed to this outlook? Are there any "hermeneutical intersections"? The challenge at this stage is to avoid any

20. Pollefeyt, "Hermeneutical-Communicative Religious Education," 15.

appearance of passing judgement; rather, the believer is encouraged to ask questions to draw out the opinions of the interlocutors.

In the second phase of "setting in motion," Pollefeyt suggests offering something illuminative to the conversation. Sharing one's experience as a micro-narrative is not as quickly dismissed as are dogmatic statements about one's faith. The believer can say, for example, in first-person, "I believe this . . . " without making dogmatic statements such as "The Catholic Church teaches or says . . . " In this way, the believer still "owns" their own faith and experience without surrendering their convictions or regressing into syncretism. Similarly, the story or testimony might touch upon the transcendent or a personal experience in the practice of the faith.

In pre-evangelization *ad extra*, the "teacher" does not primarily function as a specialist or expert, but almost exclusively as witness. This may bring a bit of relief to the average pew-sitter. I suggest that, for many American Catholics who cannot articulate what they believe and why they believe it, one's perceived lack of knowledge can sometimes be used as a cop-out or excuse to not evangelize. However, in the role of witness, the laity have far less reason to absolve themselves.

Part of the role of pre-evangelization is to attract and intrigue the other. As a witness, the believer offers perhaps the closest nonverbal proclamation of the *kerygma* through their lifestyle and actions. The point of departure may still rest with the human experience of the nonbeliever. But instead of correlating this to the Christian tradition or faith, the response can be an exchange of experiences and beliefs. Because pre-evangelization is not catechesis or instruction in the faith *per se*, the role of a specialist or expert can remain at the parish level, whether in the person of the priest or individual in charge of the RCIA process.

So what does pre-evangelization look like practically in the so-called "real world"? In the next chapter, I will look at eight methods of pre-evangelization. These are not the only methods; however, they do illustrate various aspects of pre-evangelization which have been described in earlier chapters. Each of these examples will be analyzed against the principles of the HCM.

8

Eight Methods of Pre-Evangelization

DESPITE MY DOUBT THAT a single method exists which can adequately address the challenge of awakening or preparing nonbelieving young adults to the gospel message, I realize that clergy, pastoral workers, and Christians at large often need some guidance on how to respond to this growing group of "native nones." In this chapter, I offer eight methods which broadly illustrate the praxis of pre-evangelization. These methods are attributed to or categorized as: (1) Luigi Giussani, (2) Taizé, (3) L'Abri, (4) Nightfever, (5) Conversational Evangelism, (6) Community Service, and (7) Digital Pre-Evangelization. I have already briefly introduced some of these in chapter 6.

Acknowledging that there are a great variety of practices at a local level which may not be represented, I chose each of these methods to highlight a dimension of pre-evangelization. In some cases, the methods overlap several elements and may be considered complementary. Some of these suggested methods are formalized programs while others are approaches that are less programmatic but nevertheless may be extracted through the writing of the authors and their associated ministries or apostolates.

Given the rapidly changing world and the experiences of young adults as they grow older, any method or program can quickly become obsolete. Hence, when analyzing the effectiveness of these methods and their use today, we might consider the historical and cultural trends and shifts of American young adults over the past fifty to seventy-five years. Any method is likely to be contextualized according to the time and culture. At the same time, lessons can be learned from methods or methodologies which may feed into or strengthen the development of a new model or method. We can adapt the experiences and successes from these methods to new trends or shifts. Those in pastoral practice may cull certain ideas or approaches which may appeal to a particular group or demographic of young adults.

Luigi Guissani

Perhaps one of the earliest methods of pre-evangelization can be attributed to Msgr. Luigi Giussani (1922–2005), an Italian priest and educator who founded a movement called Communion and Liberation as a means of evangelizing young people. Guissani never explicitly uses the word "evangelization" or "pre-evangelization" in his writings; however, his influence on Popes John Paul II, Benedict, and Francis implies a certain depth, relevance, and level of importance to his method. Many of Giussani's works have been introduced by leading figures in the Roman Catholic hierarchy; namely, cardinals Angelo Scola, Josef Ratzinger, Marc Ouellet, and Jorge Bergoglio.[1]

Based on the first book of his trilogy (or PerCorso),[2] Giussani's method focuses on the recognition and stimulation of the "religious sense." This "sense" is a kind of predisposition to religious faith which Giussani believes is inherent and common to human nature. As Bergoglio states, the problem is not the existence of God but "of the human, of human knowledge and finding in humans themselves the mark that God has made, so as to be able to meet with him."[3] It is this "opening the human heart" that, I believe, corresponds to the stage of pre-evangelization, similar to how the explicit communication of the gospel of Christ corresponds to the *kerygma*, and catechesis *per se* is the intellectual and human formation which is conducted within a community of Christian believers.

Giussani's method stems from his own pastoral experience with Italian young adults in the 1950s and 1960s. Rejecting a reduction of the Catholic faith to a moralism or rigid set of rules, he became convinced that young people do not encounter God because they have never been presented the true God and because many believers within the Church do not act as

1. Several reflections on Giussani's work from these figures are included in Buzzi, *Generative Thought*. Cardinal Ratzinger presided at Giussani's funeral in 2005; his own experience with Giussani is recounted in Savarona, *Life of Luigi Giussani*.

2. The PerCorso includes *The Religious Sense* (1997), *At the Origin of the Christian Claim* (1998), and *Why the Church?* (2001).

3. Bergoglio, "For Man," 80.

authentic witnesses to God or Christ. Hence, his movement *Gioventu Studentesca* (Student Youth) focused on the formation of student leaders to act as protagonists, engaging their peers, many of which were young Communists and other secular groups at that time. Student leaders were trained to engage their peers through an anthropocentric, inductive method.

Giussani's method begins with discerning whether the individual believes in the existence of God or even a transcendent being.[4] For the Christian believer, the search for meaning may coincide with God as the beginning, end, and *telos* (or final purpose) of being and all creation. However, Giussani warns that Christians "cannot ask what the word 'God' means to someone who claims to be a nonbeliever."[5]

Therefore, the Christian tradition is not the beginning of the search. Rather, Giussani argues that the individual must begin with the self as subject. Through personal reflection, inquiry, and experience of reality as object, one is less likely to acquiesce to the mindset of the group or cultural viewpoint. Likewise, the human subject must courageously confront the existential questions about the meaning of life, including the reason for one's existence and purpose, and the afterlife. Through attentiveness to the questions that arise in the heart, one comes to understand an external presence or sign outside of oneself that beckons to a deeper meaning or purpose.[6] Giussani places great emphasis on stimulating an experience of wonder and awe, which may be generated through beauty, goodness, order, and love. Such an experience "provokes"[7] the individual to discover transcendence, even a "sense of the divine."[8] All of these experiences then become possible openings to a greater mystery.

Yet, the individual must remain open and take a reasonable risk to delve deeper into the meaning or significance of these external realities and their relationship to the subject. This active engagement leads to asking questions. The person begins to notice certain signs which refer to

4. Giussani's underlying philosophy is very Thomistic. Aquinas sees assent to God's existence and positive attributes of God as a preamble of faith (*praecedentia ad fidem*), however proofs through natural reason for God's existence are not necessarily a contingent or dependent factor toward making an act of faith.

5. Giussani, *At the Origin*, 5.

6. "Man truly affirms himself only by accepting reality and being, so much so that he gains to accept himself by accepting his existence: that is, a reality he has not given himself." Giussani, *Religious Sense*, 10.

7. Giussani, *Religious Sense*, 110.

8. Giussani, *Religious Sense*, 105.

something else. In other words, a reality whose meaning suggests another reality will lead to yet another reality.

But the individual can also fail to respond to these promptings. This passivity becomes essentially a kind of escape or evasion. He or she may hold preconceptions which block the ability to be attentive or become detached from the preformed idea.[9] For example, the person might sense or experience something which is rather provocative in the natural world and yet go no further in examining the deeper questions (e.g., Giussani uses the examples of a vase which is on the table but one does not ask who gave it or one hears a sound or voice in the mountains but one does not ask who said it). So, the individual needs to be both open and free (that is, unbound by preconceptions) to the questions which arise. Hence, Giussani's method therefore centers around individual freedom, as an antithesis of religious coercion or imposition. This may mean that, during the pre-evangelization stage, the Christian may need to intentionally prompt the unspoken questions. They must also be careful to listen to the responses without judging the nonbeliever and thereby stifling the process of conversion.

Giussani admits that an exploration of the religious sense by itself cannot determine the truthfulness of the Christian message.[10] Therefore, an encounter as a mediated revelation of the divine needs to occur. The "encounter" is a key component of Giussani's method; it is through this experience that the object imposes its reality onto the subject. Lemna and Delaney claim that Giussani leaves space for a dialogical encounter that does not require explicit reference to the person of Christ.[11] The encounter, therefore, can occur through anything physical in creation.

However, the encounter does not stand in isolation but grows fruit by "coming into being of a relationship with a person or with a community of persons."[12] In other words, while Giussani's method begins with the individual, the process continues within the larger community. He or she is continually surrounded by witnesses in the peer group, which supports the conversion process with dialogue. As Giussani notes, "Human beings generally listen more attentively to the [person] who speaks on the

9. Giussani, *Religious Sense*, 128.

10. Giussani, *At the Origin*, 35.

11. Lemna and Delaney, "Three Pathways," 47.

12. Giussani, *Morality*, 16.

basis of his own experience and criteria than to the one who speaks in the name of another."[13]

The believer in Giussani's method does not function strictly as a theological expert. While a basic knowledge of one's faith may be helpful in terms of responding to and even stimulating the kind of existential questions that emerge in the pre-evangelization process, the most critical aspect is being open to sharing from the richness of one's individual experience in the Christian faith. The protagonist of the encounter is the witness, providing the provocation of a speech, behavior, or lifestyle which may oppose a familial or cultural norm.

Giussani's method is grounded in how the human person becomes aware of and relates to the external world. He recognizes the use and benefit of the natural world as potential provocative causes of the religious search. However, his method could digress into a presuppositional approach; for example, when Giussani insists that one probe into when and how a nonbeliever uses the term "God." He suggests it is possible that the nonbeliever's opinion may be only based on what others say or believe and may have never taken the time to personally investigate or consider their own position.[14] While I believe this topic could be part of a fruitful dialogue in the pre-evangelization phase, I would caution that the progression of the discussion not turn apologetical or polemical.

Giussani's method could also be considered correlational because he advocates linking the existential questions of the human person with God, who is proposed as the only answer. As Pollefeyt argues, this method assumes that human experience can be necessarily correlated or connected with the Christian tradition.[15] Given the culture's heterogeneity and growing demise of Christian symbols, young people appear to "shut down" once the topic of Christianity is introduced. Rather, the witness should be sensitive toward a multi-correlative approach, which allows for several interpretations.

Taizé

Taizé is an ecumenical monastic community founded by Brother Roger Schutz in Burgundy, France, in 1940. The community's mission focuses on

13. Giussani, *Morality*, 131.

14. Giussani, *At the Origin*, 5.

15. Pollefeyt, "Reader Course Didactics," 25.

young adults between the ages of 17–30 years. Taizé as a method of pre-evangelization can be very attractive to young adults, as demonstrated by the number of young people from various countries who have flocked to Taizé, France, and its various manifestations in American liturgies. Manuela Casti identifies Taizé as a model for those in ministry to youth.[16]

Taizé pilgrimages are promoted through parishes and sometimes schools.[17] The environment is deliberately open in terms of audience. In a spirit of ecumenism, young people from all faiths and even "nones" are welcomed.[18] As a pilgrimage or retreat, Taizé was designed to offer an opportunity to come away from ordinary life. Simplicity in lodging and meals provide a marked contrast to the materialism in which young adults live.[19] Young persons are explicitly welcomed to the site in terms of signage and personal greeting by another of similar age. Hence, a peer becomes guide, witness, and *accompagnateur*. The communal dimension is fostered by young adults working together in teams on everyday tasks.[20]

The key distinction of Taizé as pre-evangelization is its unique approach to liturgy and prayer. Held three times per day, prayer is communal, but also brief, silent, and meditative, consisting of repetitive sung and chanted music surrounded by an atmosphere bathed in candlelight.[21] Kramer asserts that the Taizé prayer style is particularly attractive to contemporary young adults because the texts are expressive of personal emotions and common struggles; the rituals create a powerful mystical and collective experience, evoke the beauty of the arts, and create an opportunity for silence within a world filled with noise and distraction.[22] It is this stillness that stimulates the participant to empty the mind of words and ideas and rest or simply be in the presence of God. In other words, if the young person does not approach the transcendent with preconceived notions or beliefs, they may be better able to receive the kerygmatic message.

---

16. Casti, "Taizé," 43. Taylor, *Secular Age*, 517, likewise hails Taizé as an illustration of young adults' quest for authenticity.

17. Casti, "Taizé," 115.

18. All of the interviewees in Casti's study were from various Christian backgrounds, e.g., Anglican, Methodist, Mennonite.

19. Casti, "Taizé," 119.

20. Santos, *Community Called Taizé*, 24–26.

21. Casti, "Taizé," 146; Santos, *Community Called Taizé*, 41.

22. Kramer, "Filling the Spiritual Void," 43–51.

Daniele Hervieu-Léger proposes Taizé as an example of a particular religiosity defined as *pelerin* (pilgrim). It is therefore not surprising that Santos describes himself being in the Taizé atmosphere as a "pilgrim in a sea of spiritual seekers."[23] Taizé's objective is to "spiritually awaken youth" with "various levels of religious literacy" where "Christian belief can no longer be assumed" but awakened through a "journey of discovery."[24]

As pre-evangelization, Taizé's approach is personalistic but also bears a hint of the presuppositional. Casti suggests the method allows young adults to "descend into inner contradictions."[25] The witness acts as a "sign contradicting the world" and provides concrete examples of Christianity rather than focusing on theoretical arguments.[26] Perhaps what is not as strictly associated with pre-evangelization within the Taizé experience is the introduction of selected scriptural readings (called Bible Introductions) and the small group discussions on these.[27] Young adults are required to attend these groups as part of the pilgrimage experience. This would tend to suggest the introduction of the kerygmatic element. However, Casti admits that Taizé does not necessarily connect to the message of the gospel but rather, the "God of the Bible is experienced in experiential and relational forms."[28]

The Taizé method works well as a retreat-style format; however, the greater challenge in the American context is how to extract and adapt portions of its elements in the secular realm. The Nightfever method, which I describe later in this chapter, incorporates some of the liturgical elements of Taizé.

L'Abri

The L'Abri (meaning "shelter" in French) is also a retreat-style program, which began in Switzerland by Francis Schaeffer in 1955. Within the United States, the L'Abri experience is available in locations in the states of Massachusetts and Minnesota. Based upon Schaeffer's writings, its goal is to help young adults better understand their presuppositions toward religion.

---

23. Santos, *Community Called Taizé*, 40.

24. Casti, "Taizé," 97.

25. Casti, "Taizé," 98.

26. Casti, "Taizé," 107.

27. Casti, "Taizé," 120–21.

28. Casti, "Taizé," 210.

Like Taizé, young adults over eighteen apply to L'Abri locations but only a limited number are accepted for each term of stay (typically, up to two- or three-and-a-half months). While staying at the site, they are not allowed to have a job or travel within the local area. Time is devoted to a specific program of study of the individual's choice (roughly four hours per day) together with mandatory Bible study (again, four hours per day), accompanied by required collective duties to maintain the property. Similar to Taizé, the environment at L'Abri is communal, centered around a pattern of meals, walks, talks, and a Sunday church service. Such a setting is geared toward providing an atmosphere that would stimulate conversation about philosophical and religious ideas.[29]

L'Abri reflects Schaeffer's belief that, in pre-evangelization, the individual must be reached both emotionally and intellectually. Hospitality is demonstrated at L'Abri through the intentional provision of open, nonjudgmental space for one to ask questions, such that a sense of welcome and trust may grow between the nonbeliever and the Christian. L'Abri makes generous use of aesthetics, not as mere functional or utilitarian pieces but as truly representative of the creativeness of God as expressed through the human person and an image of something unseen.[30]

The dialogical element of L'Abri is similar to Giussani's. Schaeffer did not espouse beginning the conversation with dogmatic statements of the truth of the Bible or Christianity, but instead sought to lead the young adult to an awareness of the contention between the nature of the external world and the nature of the human person.[31] By asking questions, the young adult would naturally be propelled toward recognizing their inadequate worldview. However, the line of argument then diverges into a dialectic. The nonbeliever then must face the tension of recognizing that they are made in the image of God and yet are fallen because of sin. They are living in a reality created by God and yet become aware that they embrace an alternative worldview. Therefore, they are bound by presuppositions which oppose reality.

The L'Abri experience illustrates the communal and aesthetic aspects of pre-evangelization, but its conversational style is apologetical based upon presuppositions. The method seems to reflect Pollefeyt's anthropological experience model because the young person is welcomed as they are, allowing the answers to surface (therefore, a rather Socratic method).

29. Wellum, "Francis A. Schaeffer," 9.
30. See Schaeffer, *Art and the Bible*, 34–35.
31. Schaeffer, *Complete Works*, 140–41.

At the same time, the method is also correlational, contrasting the individual's presuppositions with a Christian understanding of reality. Like Taizé, L'Abri is what I would define as an intentional program, meaning that young adults must travel to a new physical location.

Alpha

Many American parishes and churches, both Catholic and Protestant, are familiar with and utilize the Alpha program as part of their overall evangelization or mission outreach. The Alpha program was begun by Nicky Gumbel, a former attorney, and John Wimber (associated with the Vineyard Movement) at Holy Trinity Brompton (HTB) in London, an Anglican Church with a "charismatic-Vineyard" church theology. Designed to be an initiatory class for new Christians at the parish, Alpha is ten-weeks in length with fifteen talks on DVD/video. Due to its success, the course was opened to nonbelievers; in 1994, HTB videotaped the fifteen talks of the Alpha Course and began selling the Alpha curriculum.[32]

Alpha is designed to allow participants to explore the validity and relevance of the Christian faith for contemporary life. It is a practical introduction to the basics of Christianity, centered around a meal (during which no religious talk is allowed; rather, it is a time for building friendships/relationships), a videotaped talk (usually by Nicky Gumbel), and small-group discussion. During this time, participants are encouraged to ask questions; no topic is off limits.

An advantage of Alpha as a pre-evangelization method is its communal environment, situated at the local parish or church. Typically, Alpha is promoted in church bulletins and occasionally in local media formats. I would argue that this form of marketing more likely reaches what can be termed "fringe" Christians, or those who are not actively practicing but who may still be connected to the local church or parish. The audience may also include those known and invited by active parishioners. Through the meals and small groups, friendships with others in a similar "seeking" mode can develop. Learning often occurs through these friendships. Gumbel's talks are lively and incorporate language which is understandable at a theologically basic level. What may be a bit humorous to young adults today are the styles of hair and dress of audience members in the videos, which can suggest that the program is somewhat anachronistic.

32. The Alpha course syllabus can be found in Heard, *Inside Alpha*, 36–37.

Several similar Alpha-like courses or programs have emerged in recent years in an effort to contextualize the basic premises of Alpha. However, these are mostly all designed to be placed in a local parish or church environment. Thus, a personal invitation or marketing toward the nonbeliever still needs to be done. Because as the gospel message is introduced in the first few sessions, I would argue that a good portion of the Alpha course would be termed more of evangelization versus pre-evangelization. By week three, the participant is encouraged to make a personal prayer of conversion. Despite many positive reviews of Alpha, based on some blogs of young adult nonbelievers and comments from one of the participants in my qualitative research, this method could be considered less effective in terms of being more programmatic and coercive.[33]

Nightfever

Many American Catholic parishes in urban areas have more recently sponsored an event called Nightfever. Nightfever was initiated by Katharina Fassler-Maloney and Fr. Andreas Süss after a similar event held in Bonn, Germany, after the Cologne World Youth Day 2005. Since then, over 3,500 Nightfever events have taken place in over 27 countries. The Nightfever method straddles the parish walls in its pre-evangelization method.

Nightfever is typically held in large cities in a location associated with a great amount of foot traffic because of local bars, restaurants, or sporting events. A Catholic Mass is celebrated first within the parish walls, but this event is peripheral to the primary goal of pre-evangelization. The church is then converted into a sanctuary, filled with candles. The Blessed Sacrament is exposed within a monstrance. The church doors are open to anyone who wishes to enter. Soft music plays in the background. Young adult Catholics serve as volunteers to invite passers-by to simply enter the church, light a candle, and place it on the altar in front of the Blessed Sacrament, or simply to sit quietly. One can also write down a prayer and slip it anonymously inside a box. One need not be Catholic or even Christian to enter the church. Priests sit quietly and unobtrusively on the sides of the church but are also available

---

33. For an interesting look at responses from young adult agnostics and atheists who have attended Alpha courses, see Leggett, "Inside Alpha." Participant R is the only interviewee in my qualitative study who indicated he had attended an Alpha course: "The Alpha course, I found to be very, just . . . it's more geared toward people that don't have a Christian background at all. But that's why . . . I mean, I still enjoyed it. I found it very welcoming."

for conversation, questions, or even confession, if a young person wishes. Young adult volunteers are available for conversation and prayer.

As a method of pre-evangelization, Nightfever employs what could be termed a liminal *ad extra* approach. Rather than passively waiting for others to enter the church, young adults actively (but not coercively) engage and welcome anyone who happens to be walking around the parish environs. Because the invitation is unexpected, the subsequent experience may generate surprise and curiosity. Similar to Taizé liturgy, the internal parish environment promotes a sense of mystery and offers an unplanned period of silence; the attendee therefore may experience the transcendent. The witness acts more on the sidelines, respecting the freedom of the visitor; he or she is not coerced to step inside the parish. Relationally, it places no demands on the visitor to engage with others once inside the parish.

"Conversational Evangelism"

Norman Geisler's "conversational evangelism" can be distinguished from the methods mentioned above by how it shifts the locus of pre-evangelization toward the secular environment, which is where I argue the majority of young adult "nones" need to be initially engaged. Geisler advocates this method as a supplement or additional tool to be used with other methods of kerygmatic proclamation.

Geisler proposes that one must first listen to the unbeliever's story, in order to uncover common ground as well as potential gaps in their understanding of Christianity. As Jesus was "the master at asking questions . . . [and] knew the value of allowing others to surface the truth for themselves," the believer should similarly probe the individual in a way that causes him to recognize his own inconsistencies and barriers to the gospel message. The conversation is crafted so the individual can evaluate the strengths and weaknesses of their personal beliefs and to come to the "right" conclusions on their own.[34] Finally, the Christian should seek to build bridges on both the cognitive and emotive levels to facilitate a direct and explicit discussion on the *kerygma*.

I would suggest that Geisler's method is a kind of presuppositional apologetics, positioned in the context of a relationship. By itself, this approach may be beneficial as a kind of initial script or prompt but it hinges on a veneer of anthropocentrism; the primary goal of the conversation appears

34. Geisler and Geisler, *Conversational Evangelism*, 26, 31.

to be less directed toward the person and more toward the kerygmatic message. It relies on a systematic approach towards engaging in conversations with others, encouraging the memorization of key questions and steps to be followed in sequential order. While this format is helpful for those lacking confidence in sharing their faith, it tends to oversimplify and reduce pre-evangelization to a formula, which leads to the evangelizer appearing less natural and the conversation somewhat contrived, overly focused on the end goal of an explicit proclamation of the gospel.

Community Service

Growing up in an age when community service was often integrated with education and required as part of the curriculum, young adults in the United States seem to both highly value and participate in activities designed to promote and improve socio-economic or psychological well-being of humanity.[35] Activities and projects which may fall under the broad category of "community service" may include, but are not limited to, serving the homeless at soup kitchens or food pantries, assisting children with literacy challenges, or aiding those suffering from natural disasters. Some of these projects may be of limited scope and audience; they may be organized by parishes and churches, connected to campus ministries or religious orders, or run by secular organizations, such as the Peace Corps. Young adults also seem to be drawn to "voluntourism," which refers to a blend of work and leisure activity, often conducted in developing countries. Because, as Nebreda suggests, those of non-Christian faiths as well as atheists share common values toward the development of humanity, the arena of social justice can often be a venue where believers and nonbelievers can easily meet and gather.[36] Illustrative of Fowler's Individuative-Reflective stage, community service alongside a new peer group may act as a brief or prolonged stimulus for young adults to reflect upon existing

35. The Corporation for National and Community Service reported that between 15.8 and 33.4 percent of Millennials in the United States volunteer. Overall in 2015, 21.9 percent of Millennial young adults volunteered compared to 14 percent of young adults in 1989; the importance and impact of social engagement is also reflected in *IL*, 27, 157, 159, 184–85; Participant K in my qualitative study mentioned a positive experience during her participation in an Alternative Spring Break organized through her university's campus ministry.

36. Nebreda, "Mission of the Society," 94–104; *IL*, 157.

assumptions and values and even negative stereotypes or preconceptions often associated with institutionalized religion.

In religious circles, community service may be referred to as outreach, social action, or "servant evangelism."[37] Although controversial because of a negative association of the utilization of social welfare activities by religious groups as a façade for proselytization, community service or charitable work without explicit proclamation of the gospel message may be regarded as pre-evangelization.[38] In harmony with the ministry of Jesus who often healed the sick and fed the hungry sometimes in conjunction with preaching but many times without, community service represents the importance of faith being expressed through external action or "good works" (Jas 2:14–17).

I would argue that unchurched young adults may more readily experience the gospel through community service because it is consistent with their epistemological framework (which I discussed in ch. 2). For example, Levinas claimed that "God can be glimpsed in the ethical experience . . . God is revealed as a trace through the face of the Other to whom the self is called to serve and love."[39] However, I would suggest that the Other may be perceived as either the agent or the recipient.

In the case of the agent, Christ is symbolically encountered through the Other who is poor, vulnerable, or in need. In contrast to the individualism, self-focus, and materialism of American culture, community service may challenge the young adult to grow in consciousness of the reality and effect of poverty in one's own country and abroad. She may feel herself being drawn out in generosity and learn empathy and compassion. While the concept or existence of God may not be consciously embraced or even entertained, dichotomies in socio-economic conditions may raise questions about theodicy as the young adult confronts the possible causes of suffering, as well as the existence of evil (even if not explicitly identified as sin), and how to respond justly. A forum for reflection in response

37. "Servant evangelism" is a term coined in 1985 by Steve Sjogren, founding pastor of the Vineyard Community Church.

38. There is some debate and tension among Protestant denominations over the connection between social action and evangelism. For example, some Protestant groups treat social action as a consequence of evangelism, while others see it as a "bridge." Others see proclamation and social action as equal partners in the transmission of the Gospel. See Stott, *Contemporary Christian*, 340. Generally, there is more agreement over the identification of this activity as pre-evangelism. Catholic teaching does not separate the two but integrates them into one mission of God.

39. Urbano, "Approaching the Divine," 50.

to the community service may stimulate the young adult to process and bring meaning to the experience.

In the case of the young adult as recipient or beneficiary, the Other may act as a silent witness of the faith. In a culture where religious language or jargon can be perceived as a micro-aggression or proselytizing, the language of the witness is primarily through action. Bloesch contends that while receptivity to the gospel cannot be forced, "good Samaritan service" can stimulate greater openness to the Christian as a person.[40] Acts of compassion and care as *diakonia* (service) may represent a kind of incarnation and demonstration of the gospel message through which the recipient may identify or link the service provider with Christ. Finally, those with limited knowledge of Jesus may identify more with his works than his words. This may be even more relevant for those young adults who may only be able to hear words expressed through the filter of any preconceptions of institutionalized religion.

Digital Pre-Evangelization

In some ways, I think that digital pre-evangelization is still in its infancy, similar to the use of the printing press in the 1500s. At the same time, the use of the internet, mobile phones, and new media has already spurred an explosion of possibilities for this purpose. Obviously, the plethora of sites and apps which already exist make it impossible to evaluate all methods which could be categorized as "digital."

However, to respond in some way to this "medium as the message," I would like to offer several examples of digital pre-evangelization which are specifically directed to young adult audiences. First, the website BustedHalo.com seems to be targeted toward more mainstream "nones" or even liminal Catholics. The website StrangeNotions.com seeks to reach those with an atheistic outlook. Father Matthew Schneider has likewise compiled several examples of websites, blogs, and videos which I believe highlight various methods of pre-evangelization.[41]

Pre-evangelization via the internet can be approached quite passively through static content on websites, waiting for the curious young adult to alight based on relevant search terms. On the other hand, the digital world offers possibilities to create a participatory, interactive space for young

---

40. Bloesch, *Theology of Word and Spirit*, 240.
41. Schneider, "Applying Six Offline Models."

adults. Because digital communication has enlarged an understanding of community, numerous opportunities exist to establish virtual relationships with others. Questions can be raised, answers given, and discussions logged as reference material for other seekers. In some cases, I question whether a true "I-Thou" relationship with depth can be cultivated or whether it may be shallow and contingent upon "likes." In the digital world, this factor may be less relevant to young adults, who may reveal information and pose questions with greater trust than in a face-to-face setting. The witness (whether the website author, blogger, or intermittent poster) may need to act as both specialist and moderator, depending on the nature of the interlocutor or audience on a broader scale.

But, at a fundamental level, what is attracting or drawing American young adult "nones" to seek the Catholic Church? The qualitative research that I conducted with twenty-four unbaptized young adults may be considered both observational and illustrative of these methods. The following chapter will reveal their experiences.

9

Voices of Young Adult Catechumens

WHAT DO YOUNG ADULTS without a religious background say about their own journey toward the Catholic Church? The responses may be surprising. In this chapter, I include excerpts from interviews with twenty-four unbaptized young adults in the Archdiocese of Detroit (Michigan, USA) who chose to explore the Roman Catholic faith through the RCIA process.

While the initial phase of the RCIA, known as the pre-catechumenate, is associated with pre-evangelization. I would argue that participation assumes that there has already been some preparatory work in the heart and mind of the individual. The USCCB acknowledges that those who inquire into the Catholic Church have either had contact with other persons of faith or have had a personal faith experience.[1] By examining the experiences of young adult catechumens, I hoped to better understand the factors which drew them to investigate the Catholic Church. This step is congruent with practical theology because we now turn from the theoretical framework of pre-evangelization to ask if what appears to be going on in the so-called "real world" is actually happening.

Methodology

In this micro-study, I chose to use both quantitative and qualitative methods. However, I relied more heavily on the qualitative elements to answer my primary research questions. My research sample was purposive,

1. USCCB, *Rite of Christian Initiation.*

snowball, and homogenous. Finding the participants was not easy. I first attempted to recruit participants by posting an invitation on the diocesan young adult Facebook page. After two weeks, I received only one response. So I decided to directly approach the person(s) responsible for organizing the RCIA process at the local parish. Perhaps not shockingly, I was told by some parish staff members that there were no catechumens at all in the program! I then attempted to contact all potential participants either via email or phone.

Once I received a positive response, I scheduled an interview with the participant. Interviews took place at either the parish of where the interviewee was attending the RCIA program or in an agreed upon parish location, either in a private room (with glass windows on the door) or in a public area with sufficient privacy to maintain confidentiality.

All interviews were conducted between February 2017 and February 2018. Before each interview, participants were informed both verbally and in written form about the purpose of the study. Participants could withdraw from the research at any time and without providing any reason. Each interview began by thanking the participant for his or her time, confirming that their individual identity would be protected, and explaining the reason for the interview and how the data would be used. Participants were then asked to sign a consent form and complete a brief demographic questionnaire.

Each interview lasted between five minutes to one-and-a-half hours, depending on the interviewee's willingness to share. The participants were, in general, extremely open, cooperative, and happy to share their experience. Interviews were semi-structured, meaning that each interview was based on the same outline, but I varied the wording and the sequence depending on the way the interaction with the interviewee developed. I transcribed the interviews from electronic recordings and used deductive content analysis to first apply three predetermined codes based upon my initial research. Other codes emerged as I read iteratively and these were subsequently categorized.

The data does not obviously reflect the experiences of all young adults who have participated in an RCIA program in the United States. Neither does it address (or specifically intend to include) the experiences of young adults who have participated in the RCIA but chose not to be baptized, for whatever reason. Still, the findings do highlight certain issues, experiences, and questions that may be indicative of a broader group of young adults who share the demographic, ethnic, and socio-economic profiles of this research sample.

Demographic Information of Participants

The table below indicates the gender, marital status, ethnicity, educational level of the participants. The average age was 27.4 years. However, overall participant age ranged from 20–35.

Table 9.1 Demographic Analysis of Participants

	Count	%
Male	7	29%
Female	17	71%
Single	11	46%
Married	13	54%
Asian	1	4%
Black	2	8%
Latino	1	4%
White	20	83%
Some high school	1	4%
High school diploma	1	4%
Some college	6	25%
College certificate	2	8%
Associate	2	8%
BA/BS	11	46%
MA/MS	1	4%

Religious Background of Participants

I began each interview by asking the participant to describe their religious or spiritual beliefs before choosing to participate in the RCIA process. I wanted to understand how the participant self-identified in terms of their own religious beliefs or spirituality and to explore the presence and practice of a religious faith during the participants' childhood and teenage years. The responses would also determine if religious faith was being passed down to subsequent generations.

Table 9.2 Religious Background of Participants

	Count	%
Some belief in God	11	45.8
Spiritual	4	16.7
Christian	4	16.7
Undefined	5	20.8

The above identifiers were not prompted verbally or via survey during the interview. While none of the participants had been baptized prior to the interview, the identifier of "Christian" may be a bit unexpected. Stetzer, Stanley, and Hayes note that some unchurched young adults identify with a denomination or faith group because of their childhood behavior. They argue that this group tends to be more likely to believe that God exists, that the Christian God of the Bible exists, and that the existence of God should impact their lives.[2] In addition, they may be more predisposed and receptive to outreach efforts, organized religion, and traditional views.

None of the young adults self-identified as agnostic or atheist or expressed doubts about the existence of a transcendent, higher being, or God. As this study was very limited in size and demographics, it is certainly possible that the young adults who responded to this question did not wish to self-identify as such out of fear of judgment by the interviewer. It is also possible that, out of all the young adults who were initially approached and asked to participate in this study, only those who had a basic notion of God or spirituality responded to this study.

2. Stetzer, *Lost and Found*, 26.

Religious Background of Participant's Family

In twelve (or 50 percent) of the cases, participants identified their parents as Catholic. In three of these cases, both parents were identified as Catholic, while in nine cases only one parent was described as Catholic. When only one parent was described as Catholic, the gender was fairly equally split, i.e., four fathers and five mothers. In such cases, the marriage could be described as interfaith or "mixed faith."[3] Fifteen (58.3 percent) of the participants mentioned a parent or parents identified as "not practicing." In two of these cases, the nonpracticing parent was also described as a "believer" or "spiritual." Several participants identified their parents (or other family members) as "Catholic" even though they later added without prompting that the same parent or parents do not actively practice or only attend sporadically (e.g., Christmas and Easter, weddings and funerals).

What was more insightful is that twelve (50 percent) of the participants identified their grandparents (one or both) as either "religious" or described the grandparent in some way as actively practicing a religious faith through traditional markers (e.g., going to church, praying the rosary, display of religious items on a wall). Of these twelve, nine of the participants specifically identified a grandparent as "Catholic;" four cited their grandparents as "religious." In eight of the twelve cases, a grandmother was specifically cited as having some type of influence on the participant.[4]

These figures by themselves may suggest that the young adults interviewed are in the second generation of nonreligious or nonpracticing parents. In nearly all the twelve cases, the so-called "religious" grandparents did not appear to pass down the practice of the faith to the parents of the participants. Out of the eight "Catholic" grandparents, either the participant's father or mother or both parents were not actively practicing. In only two cases where the grandparent was "Catholic" was the parent (father) mentioned as being somewhat religious or the participant observed him praying.

As an example, Participant M mentions, "I remember my dad reading the Bible. But . . . as a kid, they never really . . . you know, they stressed that there was a god but there wasn't . . . we never had a background." In another case, the grandmother was described as Catholic but chose to raise her

---

3. Five participants (20.8 percent) described their parents' marriage as "mixed faith." Of these, two were Catholic/Orthodox, one was Catholic/Buddhist, and two were Catholic/none.

4. The "significant role played by grandparents in conveying faith and values" is confirmed in *IL*, 12.

children in the Baptist faith. While the participant did not indicate which set of grandparents was "Catholic" or "religious," there is a clear trend that the familial or native faith was not being passed down. The above phenomenon may point to a growing "lack of collective memory" among American generations since the 1960s when the participants' parents, in these cases, grew up and married. The young adults in these interviews would therefore represent the second generation in which faith is not transmitted or practiced.

Self-choice

What I found more disturbing was the admission by seven participants that their parents had allowed them to choose their own religion. The gender breakdown of these seven participants was four male and three female; within my study, gender does not appear to be a factor in this phenomenon. Among these seven participants, two indicated that their parents were both "Catholic."

According to Participant B, his Catholic but nonpracticing parents "very much wanted me to have a little bit of exposure to make my own decisions and my own determinations about, if I wanted to follow a faith or if, you know, I didn't believe in that. They were very big on me making my own decisions." Similarly, Participant C noted that her "[adopted] parents were Catholic but they never pushed it on us, like never ever. It was always our choice."

Four participants cited only one parent as "Catholic." Participant I related that he had a Catholic father but his mother:

> wasn't too terribly religious. Her parents were [religious] but they never got into the Catholic faith. I was kind of torn. I went with my dad and he wanted me to be Catholic and baptized and everything but my mom wanted me to be able to choose. So it wasn't that I wasn't a believer but it wasn't really . . . emphasized in my family, just because my parents . . . my mom wasn't practicing. So they didn't make it a point to practice the faith with the family, because of the different views, I guess.

Participant Q pointed out that his father was "religious" and baptized Protestant, yet:

> kind of thought of [baptism] . . . didn't mean anything to him. But he was so young, like he didn't even know. Like, he kind of wanted it to be like mine and my brother's choice . . . at the time that we

decide, you know, that that's actually what we want, you know, like, we fully understand what we're doing.

Participant X's comments seem to indicate that his father was reluctant to impose a specific faith on his son because of his own experience as a child:

> My mom didn't grow up in a religious family. My father though did grow up in a religious family. He went to Mass every single week. He went to Catholic school all the way through high school. But when I, like, around second grade, I noticed all my friends were getting, you know, communion and stuff and talking about church. I'm like, "Well, I don't do that." I asked [my parents] about it and my dad basically said he felt very pressured as a kid to be very involved in the Church and Catholic schools and stuff like that and he didn't want us to feel pressured. He would rather we have the choice when we were old enough to make it.

As I described in chapter 2, this phenomenon may reflect a growing trend of individualism or consumerism in religious choice. It also affirms the findings from the recent Synod on Young People that "adults are not interested in conveying the founding values of our existence to younger generations."[5] While parents did not want to appear to coerce their children to believe in a particular faith, four of the participants indicated some level of frustration because they lacked knowledge or felt "left out" when it came to religion or faith.

Religious Practice—Church

While all twenty-four participants in the study had been unbaptized, one-fourth to one-half of all participants indicated that they had previously participated in behavior traditionally associated with religious practice. Twelve participants indicated they had attended a church service in some fashion. Specifically, five of these young adults mentioned attending a church (whether Catholic, some Protestant denomination, or nondenominational) for a wedding and/or funeral. Three specifically cited attending church for Christmas and Easter only.

Interestingly, seven young adults mentioned they had taken part in some type of para-church or church-related small group. None of these

5. *IL*, 14.

groups were specifically identified as Catholic but were either Protestant or nondenominational Christian. These groups were cited as a Bible study or after-school church gathering. Many of the young adults expressed positive feelings toward these groups, which they had attended during their childhood.

Four of the participants cited memories of attending a small faith-based group during childhood. Participant Q, who grew up Wesleyan and nondenominational, describes going to church:

> Wednesday nights they would have like games and stuff at the church and they would have like a little . . . like certain parents and stuff would come in and they would teach the kids like a little Sunday session, but it was on Wednesdays and stuff. So I attended that. We didn't actually go every single Sunday or every single Wednesday. We were kind of like . . . sometimes we were busy or whatever. So, I mean, my parents . . . my dad was definitely dedicated to the church. But like maybe not as much as, you know, we probably should have been. So I had a good foundation when I was younger . . .

> When I was in elementary school, I had a girlfriend that I hung out with and she would go to a Bible study every Tuesday and I used to go with her . . . it was called Sunbeams . . . I don't think it was Catholic. I was in like second or third grade . . . I had a good time. (Participant W)

Participant L indicated she had:

> been to Sunday School as a very small child but not because my parents wanted me to go there. It was because it was an afterschool activity where a bunch of other kids were. So I just hung out and did crafts and never memorized anything or knew what was going on.

Small groups also seemed to have an impact on some of the participants during their young adulthood. In these participants' experiences, the groups seem to provide a greater sense of community than the Sunday service. Reflecting on her experience with a Catholic parish at a major university, Participant K recounts that she:

> did a few Alternative Spring Breaks and that helped me get closer to God in that way and more curious about the religion . . . I did Bible Study and just participated in different things at church and

just on campus with students. So that resonated more with me because there were more people my age and more discussions.

While Participant C said she attended services at a local Presbyterian
church, she admits:

> What's funny is I would go to Sunday service but more than the
> Sunday service, I would go to the smaller like Bible study, the
> smaller groups. So that's one of the things I did the most, which is
> odd, but I guess I felt more engaged than in the . . . I guess, versus
> the traditional church setting.

Similarly, Participant G mentioned she had attended a "support group in
the church that I went to, which was . . . you went almost into a family,
which I really enjoyed. Very supportive."

These comments suggest that, in terms of pre-evangelization, nonbelievers may be more attracted to opportunities where they can get practically involved in making a difference in the world, talk about issues that
affect them, and build relationships.

Religious Practice—Prayer

Prayer was the most common behavior associated with religious practice
mentioned by the young adults in this study. Seven expressed that they had
prayed in some manner, primarily in response to a difficulty in their lives,
whether an illness of a family member or friend.

Two participants indicated a kind of vague practice without attribut-
ing a particular meaning or purpose to the action. As Participant X simply
states, "I've always prayed to God." Participant K, whose parents were interfaith (i.e., Catholic mother and Buddhist father) claims she "would always
pray and do the Rosary and stuff, like even when I was little." Because she
does not have many memories of attending a Catholic church, she could
have been taught traditional Catholic devotions by her mother or may even
have been imitating her mother's behavior.

Upon reflection, Participant D seems surprised that she spontaneously reaches out to something beyond her for assistance with a friend:

> I had this friend, he was older than me, and he had ran [sic] away
> from home and . . . all I think could think about was just, like,
> wanting him safe, you know, and I caught myself praying. I caught

myself like . . . wow, I hope he's okay. Make sure he's okay. You know, stuff like that.

I asked her if she was consciously addressing these thoughts to "someone" or if she knew what she was doing. She responded:

I mean now that I know who [God] is, I can look back and say "yeah." But I think, like at the time, just knowing that I needed to pray for him. And that's the word I use now. But really at the time, it was just probably me thinking, thinking about my friend. But thinking about it now, I think I was praying for him. And that's kinda when I was like, well, wow, I'm praying on my own.

Participant A's brother was suffering from cancer together with mental issues and was also described as an atheist. Her brother had asked for help from the family but because she considered that there was not much that could be done for him, she determined to pray for him.

Participant P seems to diminish the method in which she prays: "I've always prayed to him. Not in a, I guess, I don't want to say, the correct way, but I always thought about him. Like making a decision and things like that." Yet, prayer is a way that she expresses her dependence on God. During marriage preparation with her fiancé, she even discovered through a questionnaire that she relies more on God in difficult times than does her fiancé.

Participant Q likewise expresses a desire for guidance as his spiritual journey proceeds: "I just asked God, like if this is what you want from me . . . 'give me peace.'" It is this sense of peace, he later describes, that gives him confidence to attend the RCIA program at his parish.

The experiences of prayer described above are primarily requests for assistance, either for oneself or another for whom the participant cares. Nevertheless, the participants' behavior demonstrates an awareness of a transcendent that listens, heals, comforts, and guides. In some ways, the attitudes toward prayer support Smith's theory of Moralistic Therapeutic Deism.[6] At the same time, this rudimentary level of communication with God can be built upon during the pre-evangelization stage. The believer might, for example, ask the young adult to describe who he thinks God is, which helps the individual begin to articulate or at least formulate a concept of the transcendent.

6. Smith's Moralistic Therapeutic Deism is briefly mentioned in ch. 2. For more detail on this theory, see Smith and Denton, *Soul Searching*, 163–71.

Attitudes Toward Catholicism

I next asked participants to tell me what had led up to their decision to attend or participate in the RCIA process. Several young adults articulated a continual curiosity about the Catholic faith since childhood, which disturbingly does not become addressed until the encounter with a significant witness in their life. The primary negative feelings expressed during this study revolve around young adults feeling "left out," "lacking knowledge," "lacking a connection," as well as feeling judged.[7] Putting these comments into context with other statements made by these same participants, it is more likely that negative perceptions of and presumptions about Christianity or Catholicism may have fueled these emotions.

Curiosity

Thirteen (54 percent) of the young adults interviewed indicated they had been curious about Catholicism on some level prior to attending RCIA. Many of these responses illustrate a kind of passivity on the part of the participant towards seeking information. By this, I mean that the individual only begins to acknowledge and give voice to the questions within after he or she is prompted by a witness outside of the familial environment.

As Participant V explains, "I never really understood it. I just know that it's always been around me. I never really . . . I just never stepped forward into it." Participant Q likewise relates, "I really didn't pursue too much on my own. Like, I was a little bit more so than my brother, like, on my own time. I would, you know, like look up things and what not."

Some young adults, however, did actively choose to investigate their persistent questions. Participant L recalls, "I actually tried reaching out to different people and different groups in my freshman year of college." However, Participant A's request to learn more was met with refusal. As she describes, "I had friends that were Catholic and I asked to go to Mass with them. They told me no." This single negative experience seemed to push her away from God for some time.

These responses suggest that religious curiosity may not be explicitly expressed and thus become latent in the young adult. Questions may fly under

---

7. Kinnaman and Lyons note that 87 percent of young adult "outsiders" use the term "judgmental" to describe contemporary Christianity. Kinnaman and Lyons, *unChristian*, 180.

the radar or become submerged under the pressing demands of life decisions (e.g., university, job or career searches and development, establishment of marriage and family) that are encountered in young adulthood. Some of these factors are specifically mentioned by the participants as being the types of obstacles they meet when seeking information about the Catholic faith.

As discussed in chapter 2, young adults may be hesitant to discuss religion or spirituality, particularly in a culture which may be indifferent or hostile toward the topic. The above responses might serve to embolden and motivate Christians to be more intentional in approaching others in the stage of pre-evangelization without the fear of being rebuffed or ignored.

Lack of Knowledge

Ten participants openly expressed a lack of knowledge about Christianity and specifically Catholic religious beliefs or practices. In some cases, the young adults felt they did not understand God, Jesus, and Mary or specific teachings of the Church. As Participant E says, "I just never knew what it was all about . . . kind of the ins and outs. How to get into heaven and all of that." In another case, a participant felt uncertain because she was unfamiliar with Catholic liturgical practices, such as knowing what to do during the Mass. This lack of knowledge may be connected to a sense of fear of asking questions, which may stem from fear of being perceived as ignorant.

A sense of relativism, or at least fluidity among denominations, emerges from several interviews; however, this could also stem from lack of knowledge. For example, Participant Y states, "I think it's very important to find a faith where you feel at home, 'cause God is home. And make sure that you are 100 percent dedicated to him like he is to you. Find a religion where you feel that way."

Often, the participants linked their lack of religious upbringing with their lack of knowledge. While Participant L had attended a Sunday school type program as a child, she had "never memorized anything or knew what was going on. So I never really learned anything as a child." Despite her "Catholic" parents and occasionally attending weddings and funerals, Participant P seems to lament, "I just really didn't know exactly what was going on. I just knew that we would do a song and things like that, but I never really knew, like, the structure of Mass or anything like that."

Sometimes the lack of knowledge was an amalgamation of several topics. Participant Q had attended both Wesleyan and nondenominational churches but was unfamiliar with Catholicism, and perhaps even Christianity in general.

> Even back then I hardly had any idea about Catholic. I barely even knew that it was, like, another part of it . . . and I really had no idea that there was so many different styles of Christianity, like how many denominations there are . . . Back then, I didn't really understand, like, the whole entirety of the church. And like, you know, salvation through Jesus Christ and, like, stuff like that. (Participant Q)

The RCIA process was viewed positively as a means of learning more, not necessarily to commit or convert to the Catholic Church. For example, after having attended a Catholic parish with his wife and children for some time, Participant G states that he "enjoyed the homilies. I really enjoyed what I was being taught. I just didn't really understand . . . and I wanted to get a better perspective, so that's the reason why I'm going through the RCIA process." Participant V's parents, who were identified as "Catholic" but nonpracticing, did not raise her in any faith. She claims she "was never quite sure what exactly, or who exactly, God was and what he was calling me to do in life. So I joined RCIA to have a better understanding."

Participant P pointed out that she enjoyed RCIA because it was a forum in which she could ask questions without being negatively perceived: "I'm sitting down every Thursday and I'm learning a lot but we're talking and I never feel embarrassed, or like a silly question."

Perhaps these comments from young adults should not be surprising. Prothero notes that "Americans are both deeply religious and profoundly ignorant about religion."[8] Further, lack of knowledge on religious beliefs and practices may be linked to a feeling of being an "outsider."

Feeling "Left Out"

Not surprisingly, four participants either explicitly used the term "left out" or alluded to the feeling of being an outsider even during a religious service. This response was likely because they had no knowledge or familiarity with the liturgical practice. As Participant E confesses, "I always knew a little bit about what it was about, but kind of felt kind of left out. Even at weddings and funerals and stuff, I just felt left out."

8. Prothero, *Religious Literacy*, 2. This is affirmed by Pew Research Center, "US Religious Knowledge Survey."

However, three participants felt "left out" specifically because of not being able to participate in the Eucharist or Holy Communion during the Catholic service. Within the Catholic Church, unbaptized persons are not allowed to share in this sacrament based upon a combination of teaching in Sacred Scripture, tradition, and canon law.[9] This may represent a perceived high boundary or barrier in terms of formal participation which may either seem insurmountable or, conversely, a goal to be attained.

For example, Participant X remembers "around second grade, I noticed all my friends were getting communion and stuff and talking about church. And I'm like, well, I don't do that." While Participant G went to Mass with his wife and children, he chose not to receive communion: "My kids would ask me why. I asked myself why," he relates. "Like, why don't I get to enjoy that, and be part of that that process?" Similarly, Participant P recalls, "I just knew that I could never go up for the Body of Christ. That was something that I never really knew what was going on."

Such comments may point more to the feeling of being an outsider with a corresponding desire to be included within the community. What is less clear from these statements is whether the young adults are simply "longing for belonging" or if they are beginning to feel a distinction between their own beliefs and the teaching and practices of Catholic Church.

Negative Perceptions of Christianity

Three participants mentioned a negative experience with Christianity or those identified as Christians. The overall feeling expressed in these narratives is that of being an outsider, being judged by another person or by images, or not feeling welcomed by the community. The underlying feeling may be that the individual is not "good enough" or "doesn't fit in" with the communal norm.

Participant L described a negative atmosphere of church based upon religious images which she perceived as judgmental or condemning.

9. The Catholic Church interprets numerous passages from John 6 to mean that Christ's true body and blood is "truly, fully, and substantially present" under the species of bread and wine in the Sacrament of the Holy Eucharist. Consequently, the Church interprets 1 Cor 11:29 to mean that the reception of Christ's Body and Blood consciously without faith would be sacrilegious. Further, *CIC*, c. 912, states, "Any baptized person not prohibited by law can and must be admitted to holy communion." The Church, however, does permit nonbaptized persons to approach the Eucharistic table to receive a blessing from the priest.

> I was volunteering one summer in college in Oklahoma and I stayed in a church building and there were religious pictures and crosses and Jesus. And it honestly made me feel uncomfortable. I felt like I was not good enough and I was being watched. And like all these eyes were on me. Like there was something wrong with me. Just the pictures of, like, Jesus and the angels and everything. I didn't even know what they were for or what they represented but I just felt uncomfortable. 'Cause honestly I had never been around it and had never been taught anything about it.

While religious or sacred art and images can sometimes have a positive role in pre-evangelization, in Participant L's case, they can also evoke negative emotions. This suggests that the meaning of art or images according to the spectator is not neutral but becomes filtered through one's experiences or preconceptions. In other words, art and images can portray an angry, condemning God or a merciful, loving God depending on how the person already views God or religion.

Participant L also seems to associate religion with coercion or something that is forced upon another because of an event from her preteen years.

> I babysat kids when I was, like, twelve or thirteen. And the people . . . I think they were Jehovah Witnesses . . . were at the door. They actually came to the door when the parents of the two babies that I was watching weren't home and they asked if they could come inside. And I said, "No, this isn't my house, the parents aren't here" and they actually pushed open the door and came inside without my permission and attempted to make me born again or something. They laid their hands on my head, put my head back, and saying all these things. I just felt like everything that I saw based on religion, not in the movies but in the real world, was extremely overwhelming and pressuring and I didn't understand it. People were trying to push things or explain things that I didn't have answers to.

For Participant D, religious persons are perceived negatively because of a judgmental attitude toward others with whom the participant identifies because of her own childhood experience of being homeless.

> I worked at Tim Horton's and there was always this Christian group that would come in for like two hours. They would have a big family, friends, and so forth. And they were rude. They were rude. And one guy, I won't forget him, he was so judgmental. We have a lot of homeless people in Chesterfield, not a lot, but our Tim Horton's

is 24-hours, so of course they would come. So when they would come, the look in his eyes was just hate and it wasn't anything. And I just assumed he was a Christian and an asshole. Like how you can look at . . . and not even just a normal person. Why would you look at someone who has less than you and push them off? It bothered me. It bothered me my whole life.

So I have that kind of empathy for other people who have nothing, that have nothing. Like, being a homeless kid . . . like, being a homeless child and living on the streets, and then being a part of this world, and I call "this world" 'cause I feel like this is one big world but a lot of different worlds in it, and being a homeless child looking in on this world, they're just good people and they don't see you. They don't want to see you, 'cause they don't have to see you, because they don't have to see you, because, like, what can I do for them? I'm just a homeless kid. So they don't do for me. And then growing up and maybe that's why I have a lot of anger towards a lot of people. 'Cause I just thought they're all assholes. You were assholes to me when I was homeless and now that I'm clothed you want to be nice to me. It bothered me, it really bothered me. I just associated Christians with being assholes because of this group of people.

While Participant D may have been especially sensitive toward persons who show scorn to the homeless, she nevertheless correlates a negative, hypocritical image of Christianity to the described incident.

Negative impressions of Christianity can similarly result from the first impression or perception of being judged or not feeling welcomed during a church visit. Participant Y describes her visit to a couple Protestant churches: "Lutheran is very . . . I went there in high school so I started with that one. I just didn't like the atmosphere . . . Like I didn't really know the people. They weren't really welcoming. I also did that . . . Baptist? Is that what you call them? I sat through a couple services there. Again, but it just didn't feel at home."

However, a negative experience was not confined to a denomination. Participant M recalls, "I feel like I've been to other Catholic churches . . . I felt like some other Catholic churches were, like parishioners, maybe just a little more judgmental than the parishioners at St. _____."

These depictions of so-called "Christians" may be disturbing. While believers may balk at descriptive adjectives such as judgmental, unwelcoming, and coercive as being antithetical to the gospel, real-life experiences unfortunately contribute to a continued negative stereotype of Christianity.

However, what is encouraging is that these impressions can be offset and even reversed through an encounter and connection with a witness (either individual or communal) who demonstrates an authentically lived faith.

Lack of Connection

In some cases, the inability to find a church home stemmed more from indirect, occasionally vague factors. For example, six young adults used phrases such as "lacked a connection" or "nothing stuck" in relation to their experiences attending various religious services or denominations.

Two participants did not resonate with an experience with non-Christian religions. In Participant K's experience, she had attended a Buddhist school and had learned prayers and related practices, but she said she and her family "don't go to temple here. There's a Sri Lankan Buddhist temple in _____. But we go once a year maybe, just for New Years. So we don't really go much. And I don't know, I've never really connected with it much."

Participant L, who had been previously married to a Muslim, claimed she "never converted because I just never felt that I found something that I could feel connected to . . . so I don't know what it exactly was I was looking for or waiting for."

While this kind of "church shopping" provided an opportunity to discover nuances in religious denominations, it still does not seem to offer the connection that the young adults in my study are seeking.

> There were a lot of different churches that we went to. Not a whole lot really struck me in that portion of it. I know some were more about the music and spirituality of it. And some were more strictly by, by the look. But nothing really stuck in my mind from those. It's just . . . just had to dress up. And I don't even know why. It was just there. I just wanted to know why. (Participant E)

> I would go to church with [my grandmother] occasionally. And throughout the years, I went to a couple different churches, just like with some friends, to try to see what was going on. Nothing really stuck. I didn't really have a purpose, to really want to go. (Participant G)

Participant Z tried to associate with the faith of her mother and grandmother but discovered she did not share the same attraction or affinity. "Because my mom, she was baptized Lutheran and her mom goes to a Lutheran church, so I did investigate some of that, but I didn't really connect as much as I would have wanted to."

While I did not probe these young adults for the reasons for the disconnections described, it is possible these young adults simply did not form a strong relational bond with anyone within these religious communities during the times they attended.

Too Busy for God?

Five young adults alluded to the busyness of life as obstacles toward actively pursuing the RCIA program. Two of these responses related to the time commitment involved in completing education at a university. Participant K, whose mother is Catholic, stresses, "My mom was always urging me to do the RCIA program but . . . I never did it in college just because I was so busy and didn't have the time to think about it."

Similarly, Participant W struggled with time commitments. "Before we got engaged, I was full time in nursing school and I had a year off so I was, like, I might as well start and go to church, 'cause I have a year off of school, before nursing school, so I was just gonna go into that and I happened to get engaged and so, then it just kind of kicked it into perspective for me."

For Participant T, a transient lifestyle due to job obligations seemed to prevent her from making a commitment to a parish. She explains that she had "been going to Mass with my husband for nine years or so now as a couple and we've also been very transient . . . we move a lot because of school, so I never felt like I was settled, sort of like this was my home or this was my church."

For two participants, the time commitment associated with raising children was viewed as an impediment toward looking into the RCIA process. Participant C remembers that she had "kind of let it pass and at the time, about two years ago, I had an infant and two one-year olds. So you know it was . . . it would have been tough to try to do the RCIA process at that time because it's tough now." Likewise, Participant X states that "It was a busy summer, you know, the kids were all home . . . you know, vacations and stuff. I brushed it off."

The above responses may affirm that young adults tend to delay making decisions about religion due to distraction with pursuits such as attending a university or raising young children. Yet other young adults simply felt they were not ready to make the commitment of attending the RCIA program or even look for answers to satisfy their religious curiosity. In the case of Participant N, she had made friends with a Catholic coworker during her teen years. The friend had invited her to his parish but, as she states, "I realized it was some kind of like . . . class. I never went back. I was too young. I was, like, seventeen."

Lack of support was cited as a reason for putting the search on hiatus. Participant N describes getting engaged to her now-husband, who is Lutheran. Because of his religious background, she demonstrates some level of enthusiasm for learning more about and practicing the Lutheran faith:

> So it's like, oh, well ok, then maybe I'll do the Lutheran thing. You know, 'cause I'm like, we can all be Lutheran, we'll be fine. Well, he told he didn't want to go to church, like he grew up, Lutheran, private school, private Lutheran school and he's like, "I'm done." So it's like, well I don't want to do this by myself and you're not gonna support me. And I kind of left it at that.

The Role of the Witness

Each of the twenty-four participants indicated the presence of a witness in their life prior to entering the RCIA process. In twenty cases, multiple witnesses were cited as being instrumental in the participant's life. The most frequently mentioned witnesses were friends and in-laws (i.e., father-in-law, mother-in-law, future father-in-law, future mother-in-law, or a combination of these). The next most common witness was grandmother and fiancé(e) at 29.2 percent and 20.8 percent, respectively. However, the presence and witness of the grandmother appeared to be more part of the participant's childhood as a (mostly positive) memory and as a connection to the Catholic faith.

Roles of Friends and In-Laws

In ten cases (41.7 percent), the witness and support of future or current in-laws served as a positive parental role model in the participant's spiritual journey. Smith and Snell point to the importance of religious socialization with nonparental adults in the absence of highly religious parents as highly influential in the faith of teenagers as they transition to young adulthood.[10]

10. Smith and Snell, *Souls in Transition*, 234, 285.

Here, I suggest that the introduction into a new social network of relationships through dating, engagement, and marriage may facilitate a similar interaction of surrogate spiritual parenthood which counteracts the participant's nonreligious or nonpracticing parental background.

Eleven participants mentioned at least one friend who had influenced them in their spiritual journeys. Friends were all described as "devout," "religious," or "very religious." Two friends personally invited the participant to join them in attending the RCIA. As Participant Z recounts, "My best friend . . . she said, 'Hey, do you want to go to church?'" She seems to instantaneously accept as she continues, "Like why not, let's go check it out!"

While the friend and coworker of Participant M was described as both "pretty religious" and growing up "in a religious household," the friend decided to attend RCIA simply to learn more. "She knows about my background, like I was never baptized but I had thought about it. And so she said, 'Hey, I'm going through RCIA and are you interested in it?'"

The role of the friend in the pre-evangelization process seems to point to the importance of a close relationship in which trust and openness is involved. The friend-witness knows the participant intimately and undoubtedly has made an impression through conversation and lifestyle. Through the lens of friendship, the extended invitation to attend a church service or RCIA may be viewed less as a gimmick or proselytizing.

Role of the Grandmother

Several participants mentioned the presence of a grandmother who served as a witness of religious faith. However, their descriptions of their grandmother depict what may be termed a traditional figure in the practice of Catholicism. For example, the grandmother is seen praying on her knees; her room is decorated with religious objects; she reads' the Bible and explains religious figures to the participant as a child. One participant carries a rosary from her great-grandmother, which is special to her even if she does not know what to do with it. In some cases, the grandmother figure is replaced by an older neighbor or a coworker who would be the participant's grandmother's age.

The grandmothers acted as witnesses primarily for participants when they were children. The grandmother took the child to church, talked about faith (including her personal journey), read the Bible, discussed biblical stories and characters, and answered questions about the faith. For example, Participant D recounts a visual memory of her grandmother and how it impacted her:

> My grandma . . . is Catholic and she was a really devoted Catholic. Like, the most Catholic woman I've ever met. And when I would go [to her home] . . . I would watch her pray . . . every night she would pray her Rosary, on her hands and knees. And I would just watch her. It was . . . interesting.

While this young adult finds her grandmother's behavior fascinating, at the same time she sees her grandmother as an archetype or even stereotypical personality of a religious person. She wonders whether she will fit in as a Catholic because she views her own personality as somewhat more raucous or "rough around the edges" than her quiet, pious grandmother. In her journey, the grandmotherly witness in her life who sports a tattoo and rides a Harley Davidson motorcycle serves as a refreshing contrast, which seems to encourage and comfort her. She becomes satisfied that she can become Catholic and not be forced into a mold.

Roles of Fiancé and Spouse

Seven participants indicated a fiancé or fiancée as being influential. An additional two participants indicated that they had begun attending Mass with their fiancé/fiancée prior to getting married but had not begun attending the RCIA until after their marriage. This may indicate that the participant had not considered Catholicism until he or she was preparing to get married. As Participant I relates, "I met my fiancée and she was, her family was, religious or practicing. So, that was the motivator to say maybe this is the time."

When a spouse was cited as being influential in the decision to formally seek information on Catholicism, four out of five participants were female. This may suggest that the religious or religiously practicing male spouse may be more influential in the conversion of a female spouse versus the situation where the female spouse is religious. However, because my study included more female participants than males, I cannot draw a firm conclusion.

Role of Priest

Only three participants specifically mentioned a priest in the role of witness. In the two cases where the parish priest is perceived positively by the participant, the encounter with the priest takes place after the participant has already been in a stage of pre-evangelization. During his first visit with a Catholic priest as part of marriage preparation, Participant E described his initial conversation as "enlightening." As Participant S proclaims, "Fr. _____ is amazing. He makes you inspired to want to do better for yourself and for others. So I guess he is a big help, too."

The low number of participants who mentioned a priest as being influential at this stage may reflect a power differential. From an outsider perspective, it may be daunting or intimidating to approach a priest out of fear of judgement or lack of knowledge.

A negative experience with a priest is reflected in Participant L's comments: "I had a lot of questions for the priest and he, I don't know . . . I think it was because of age, like he thought if I was old enough to understand certain concepts or if they really didn't know how to explain something to me but they could never answer my questions." Clearly, she is seeking answers, yet when she does ask questions, he appears to brush her off. Such an experience may affirm some of the reasons why young adults are not attracted to religious institutions.

However, the relatively few cases of interaction with a priest as a witness may also be due to a growing shift in the primary environment in which pre-evangelization takes place. While many of the participants in this study mentioned attendance in a church or church-related small group prior to attending the RCIA, in nearly all the cases, the critical conversations and encounters take place outside the parish in a secular setting.

The witness may sometimes serve as a catalyst to reverse a previously negative view of Christianity or Christians in general. As Participant D relates: "When I got out of high school, I saw a lot of hypocrites. People that would go to church but . . . they were such assholes. And I hated that. And that's how I judged Christians, as assholes. I really did . . . and then it wasn't until I met [name of witness] that I learned that . . .um . . . not all Christians are assholes [laughter]."

Earlier in this chapter, I mentioned this young woman's negative encounter with individuals in her work environment who had identified themselves as Christians. Remarkably, when she encounters only one individual who makes a positive impression, she makes a positive correlation of this witness with Catholic Christianity. Thus, the behavior of the witness seems to serve as a kind of antidote to an earlier negative perception.

In Participant D's narrative, the witness was identified profession-ally as a "trainer," in the sense that she was responsible for orienting and teaching her younger protégé in a new job position. However, "trainer" seems to be an equally apt word for the spiritual guidance which this wit-ness provided to the participant. She teaches the young woman how to see God working in her past experiences and daily life and how to bring ordinary human concerns to prayer.

In some cases, the witness or witnesses serve as a kind of role model of Catholic Christianity. The young adult identifies a trait or lifestyle of witness which is perceived as attractive and contrasts this against a native family situation or Christian stereotypes.

> She taught me what kind of woman I wanted to be and the kind of wife I want to be, and that in order to be the kind of woman and wife I want to be, I have to listen to God. And he will guide me into those ways. 'Cause she's like my total role model that I always wanted as a little girl. (Participant D)

While the young adult may relate to the witness in terms of socio-economic level, work, lifestyle, etc., the age of the witness as role model appears to be a less relevant factor. Such responses affirm the importance of a positive witness of Christianity, and specifically Catholicism, in the individual's life.

Methods of Pre-Evangelization

What did the witness do (or not do) when interacting with the nonbeliever? Based upon the participants' responses, the believer was open to sharing their faith, personally invited the participant to a church or RCIA program, took time to answer questions, engaged in nonreligious conversation, and simply lived an authentic Christian life. Because this is a small sample, I would not isolate or prioritize any of these methods, but rather suggest that the believer as witness often demonstrates a combination of methods.

Openness to Sharing Faith

For Participant B, his bunkmates in the military acted as his primary witnesses. He observes their lifestyle which includes daily prayer and engaging him in spiritual conversation.

> It was just living next to them for so long. And they, just you know, every day talking about it. And every night, you know, going to bed, they'd be taking time out to pray . . . which you don't really see a whole lot of, you know, in the military 'cause people tend to kind of keep to themselves. But they were not very, you know, not very into hiding it. They were very open about it.

However, only one catechumen mentions a witness who uses the word "sin." As Participant Q relates, "She wasn't really afraid to announce her faith in front of others . . . she wasn't afraid to say to people like 'don't do that, like it's wrong, like it's a sin' . . . that kind of intrigued me, I guess, a little bit."

Personal Invitation

A crucial factor in the early conversion stage is the personal invitation to attend church or begin the RCIA process. While Participant A was rebuffed by her Catholic friends when she asked to attend Mass with them, her boyfriend (now fiancé) invited her to go to his church when he saw she was struggling to cope with her brother's illness.

Participant L illustrates a gentle, yet noncoercive, invitation by her mother-in-law:

> It was last summer. She had one of those bulletins from our church. At our house, she was flipping through it. She saw the RCIA section and she goes, "If you're interested in learning more about our faith, you don't have to convert or anything, but you can just go to these classes once a week and just ask your questions. There's someone there. There's a group of people there to support you. They're all at different stages of their lives but they're all going through the same things. And you'll probably get something out of it."

For two participants, the invitation is reinforced by the support of a close friend and relative who also intend to attend the RCIA program.

My friend that I work with . . . she's pretty religious and she grew up in a religious household. And she was going through RCIA just to learn . . . and she knew, she knows about my background, like I was never baptized but I had thought about it. And so she said, "Hey, I'm going through RCIA and are you interested in it?" And I was like, "Yeah, I am interested." And that's really how it happened. (Participant M)

In the case of Participant X, she had attended church services at the parish and had met the priest. Apparently, the priest had notified the RCIA director of the participant's interest. She laughs, "Then all of a sudden, [RCIA director] calls me one day and he's like, 'Hey, Fr. _____ told me if you're interested.' I was still coming to church and everything so I'm just like, let's do it."

In these cases, the response to the invitation appears to incite an immediately positive response. While not every personal invitation will result in such a response, it does show receptivity on the part of the young adult.

Just Answer the Questions

In seven cases, the participant portrays the witness as approachable and receptive to answering questions about religious matters. At this point, the participant may be termed a "religious seeker" who is actively engaged in the pursuit of knowledge from another who is perceived to be trustworthy and informed.

Participant G's mother-in-law was instrumental through her openness in answering questions. As he relates, "She would help explain things to me . . . she had this really nice big book that she gave me that I was able to read up on it . . . She was a key part, just explaining things so I understood them and the reasons why. If I had questions, I would go to her and she would give me an unbiased reason. And that really intrigued me."

Likewise, Participant J praises her in-laws: "If I have any questions, they help me. Along with his family . . . they never pressured me, but . . . if I've ever had questions, they're always . . . they're very open about helping me out." Participant X relates her husband's reaction to her religious inquisitiveness: "I started asking him questions constantly about [Christianity]. Just like the stories, and like . . . you know, stuff like that. And finally he's just like 'instead of, like, asking me,' he's like 'here, just read it' and he bought me the Bible." And Participant Y describes interactions with her grandmother: "I would ask a lot of questions . . . about her religion. You know, God, Jesus, and everything. She would show me the Christian book, what Christmas was about and Easter and everything. And then she would explain to me."

These positive experiences may be contrasted with those described by Participant L, which demonstrate the opposite effect. Earlier, I described how she was rebuffed by a priest during her childhood when she sought answers. While she is attending a university, she again approaches multiple individuals:

> I actually tried reaching out to different people and different groups in my freshman year of college . . . I had a friend who was a very devout Catholic named Matt and he tried to explain to me why he believed certain things but he didn't try very hard to explain it because he was a football player and he's a guy, so explaining to, like, a girl in college, like, why you believe certain things was kind of hard.

She is actively searching for answers on religion, yet she does not receive them at a level which satisfies her. In her experience, the witness appears incapable of explaining his faith in a language which is understandable to her.

In summary, young adults frequently asked questions when they were in a seeking mode for information on religious matters. As I explained in chapter 2, parishes may fail to attract or even repel this demographic if staff or parishioners are unwilling to take the time to answer these questions. The above comments also support Thielma and Twenge's research that religious organizations should be actively discussing with young adults the so-called "big questions" about God, life, love, and meaning.[11] Emery White suggests that, in order to reach the unchurched, communities of faith may need to become more comfortable with responding to questions posed by persons unfamiliar with religious language or practice. He terms these as "WT*IUWT" or "what the fuck is up with that?" questions, referencing the acronym which young adults frequently use in texting or posting on Facebook.[12] Such an environment might help "outsiders" feel welcome to ask these questions and explore the answers. He stresses that the process of evangelization includes earning a right to talk about spiritual subjects by first building relationships.

---

11. Twenge, *iGen*, 141. In Thielma's study, she also notes that all participants were able to speak with a layperson who "would answer their questions and were knowledgeable about the faith" (ibid., 29).

12. White, *Meet Generation Z*, 129–30.

In the *ad extra* environment in which the participants in this study interact, the lay witnesses who can explain a religious belief or concept along with providing what are judged as reasonable and understandable answers seem to be admired and perhaps even sought out. While the witness desires to assist the seeker and provides resources (e.g., spiritual books, Bible) at an appropriate time, he or she is decidedly noncoercive in behavior, which respects the freedom of the individual.

Conversation

Seven participants indicated a conversation with the witness or witnesses as being insightful or important in their early spiritual journey. For example, Participant B described his military bunkmates "every day talking about [religion]." Frequent conversation served to expose the participant to religious vocabulary or jargon and facilitated a comfort and trust between the witness and nonbeliever. As with the personal invitation, the young adults in this study appear to be open and receptive to a conversation about spiritual or religious topics.

Participant C admitted that she had "talked to [parish school staff member] on a regular basis and I told her I was thinking about it. And from the time I told her I was thinking about it, she just kept talking about it and encouraging it and she offered to be my sponsor."

> On the first day we [Participant D and her coworker] didn't even talk about work. All she talked about was how beautiful I was. I was like "stop it, like, you're crazy." But she wasn't talking about my looks, she was talking about . . . my life. Like "you have such a light to you. You have such a Holy Spirit." And I'm like, no, I don't.
>
> Yeah! Me and [coworker] had, like, literally formed one. It's the weirdest thing . . . she is the only person that can talk to me that I listen to. And that's weird to say. I take advice from my parents but she literally talks to my soul. Like her advice is so heartwarming, you know what I mean? So anyway, our first day, all we talked about was like . . . I told her my story about my mom and my childhood and instantly I opened up to her. It's the weirdest thing, 'cause I don't, I don't.
>
> She asked me like, like trainers do, like, "What did you used to do? Why did you come here? Are you sure you want this job?" And then literally everything just started flowing. The lady knows

everything about me. She's only known me for like six months. It's very rare, right? She knows a lot. (Participant D)

[Mother-in-law] was just a great conversationalist, I guess. So she would talk to me just about different things that were going on. (Participant G)

[Friend from high school] would always have these really deep conversations with me. (Participant L)

She wasn't afraid to talk to you about it . . . she would tell me what she believed and then I would like tell her what I believed. (Participant Q on her female friend)

She's probably one of my oldest friends. She has a really strong Catholic faith, so she's been someone I've talked to about it as well . . . I mean we've been friends for nearly twenty years. I wouldn't necessarily say "approach" but it just came up in conversation . . . so we just talked about [RCIA] a lot. She said you know if you ever have questions, or whatever. I talked to a lot of my friends and [RCIA director]. A lot of people, they knew I was with [name of fiancé] and they knew he was Catholic. They were asking me "Do you think you're going to convert?" I definitely talked to a lot of people about it before. (Participant U on her girlfriend)

The conversations with the participants in this study appear to be natural, uncontrived, and at the same time, purposive without being intrusive or coercive. They are certainly more relational than confrontational. Even in the instances above, the format appears to be more dialogical rather than proselytizing.

Lifestyle

In three cases, the participant particularly alluded to an attraction to the witness' behavior or lifestyle. Within the interview, this behavior was contrasted to an experience or behavior Participant L had with her own family.

Right after I got divorced and then I met my husband and when I was first getting to know his mom and dad and his brother and sister and just seeing the family dynamics. *It wasn't even religion that started it. It was the way that they treated each other* . . . I had never seen that kind of respect between parents and children and between brother and sister. I had never seen anything like that before. The way that I was raised, my friends, people I had grown up around. And I was wondering, like I had always wanted that family dynamic like that. What is it that holds these people to these standards, you know. And it's definitely their beliefs, it's the way they were raised. The faith that they've learned and the things that they have been taught. And I was open to absorbing as much as I could because it was just so pleasant to be around and I always wanted you know that for myself . . . I recognized something about them that I desired. (Participant L; my italics)

Speaking about his female friend, Participant Q explains, "I could tell from the first week that I knew her that she showed her faith." Later, as he gets to know her family, he expresses some trepidations due to perceiving her father as "a pretty strict Catholic." However, as he notices the behavior and interactions of her family, he is struck by something different and attractive about their lifestyle:

I saw how, you know, her dad like makes them stay after [Mass] on Sundays, like family time . . . they talk about God at the table . . . they pray a Rosary at nighttime. And I kind of was looking at that, like how they were connecting as a family. Not everything is always going to be perfect. But like I saw that, what they were doing and, you know, I kind of liked that. You know, me and my dad used to do that like sometimes at the dinner table. But it was kind of a hit or miss thing. It wasn't like an every night thing like their family does. And like, I kind of saw that and I was like, you know, that would be something I'd like to do, you know, in my family one day. So I guess just seeing her whole family connecting together like that is something that helped me.

The experience serves as a kind of positive shock or dramatic contrast which causes the individual to reflect upon his or her own perhaps latent or unexpressed desires.

She's so kindhearted and she is because she believes in Jesus so he lives through her. You feel it. You feel it, that's why people want to hate her. When she touches me, I cry. I'm not kidding, when we're in church and we're singing, and she grabs my hand, like our holy spirits are bonding. And then she kind of opened my eyes to see that I can be cool and believe in God. (Participant D)

Interestingly, very few of the participants specifically mentioned the witness explicitly speaking about Jesus. This notable absence in the narratives does not indicate that pre-evangelization should not include a reference to

Jesus. However, it may suggest that this was not the most critical or impressionable moment of the participant's conversion process.

In the case of Participant Q, the intentional visit of two outside witnesses serves to spur the participant to realize that he knew less than he realized about Christianity, which prompted him to seek more intently for answers. While he clearly had the possibility of asking the questions around the family table or with his father after church, for some reason, he did not feel comfortable doing so. Interestingly, he describes his own father as being "religious" but at the same time, does not attribute him to be a sufficiently knowledgeable authority.

The encounter features prominently in many of the participants' narratives. Two types of encounters are demonstrated in this study: (1) the encounter with a person who challenges the individual's perception or stereotype of Christians or Catholics, and (2) the encounter with a parish member or priest who helps "enlighten," encourage, or prompt one to move to a new level. In each case, the encounter appears to reverse the presuppositions and motivate the individual to shift their mindset, which launches them in a more active search for information on the Catholic faith.

Mystery and Tradition

While mystery and tradition might not seem to be attractive components for contemporary young adults, both of these factors emerged in four narratives in my study. For the male participants, mystery and tradition were represented by liturgical, sacramental, and architectural elements. Whereas for two females, the sense of mystery was conveyed through perceived coincidences, which trigger the individuals to associate and connect the active and personal presence of God within their lives.

For example, Participant B mentioned that he had attended a non-denominational church with his "Catholic" but nonpracticing parents. However, he did not find the nontraditional style of liturgy appealing. As he relates, "There's just a lot of dancing and singing and . . . that to me, but, I don't want to, you know, discredit it or anything . . . but to me personally, it just seemed to me a little hokey."

In contrast, he is attracted to and likens his positive experience in the military with the Catholic Church because of its structure and tradition.

> To me, God is something that is very much honored and respect-
> ed and, coming from the service . . . things are very ritualistic

and you do things a certain way and it just connected with me. It makes the most sense. You know, if I'm going to honor God then I'm going to do it, you know, like the way we've been doing it for the last two thousand years . . . Maybe initially, I was more pulled into it by the mystery of it cause it does seem from the outside, like not from somebody very religious . . . but it all seemed very mysterious to me and I guess that's what kind of drew me in a little bit. (Participant B)

The mystery of transubstantiation appealed to Participant Q, who grew up in both Protestant and nondenominational faiths. "I think that was probably something that intrigued me . . . probably the most. I guess just really partaking in the true body and blood of Christ. Like that was one of the biggest things that kind of, you know, pushed me towards looking more into the Catholic Church."

Aesthetics and beauty often play a role in pre-evangelization. For example, Participant R had studied French and had lived with a family in the Loire Valley during his university years. During his stay in France, he had visited several cathedrals (i.e., Notre Dame, Chartres, Sacré Coeur) and indicated he had been moved by the sense of beauty, peace, and stillness. He relates, "The atmosphere is just beautiful in there . . . it's grand but it's also very calm and somber. It just has this air of godliness to it." Here, church architecture becomes a conduit, even a sacramental, to convey both mystery and tradition. The Nightfever method, which I described in chapter 8, is designed to replicate this experience.

Mystery and tradition are similarly reflected through Participant R's attraction to a religious and historical relic displayed in a church in France. "There's one church [author's note: Chartres Cathedral] that I visited that does have the Sancta Camisa, which is what Mary wore when she gave birth to Jesus." Earlier in my interview with Participant R, he had mentioned that his family background was Quaker; however, he did not practice this faith. He later told me that he had no desire to practice this faith in the future. As this confessional belief typically eschews ornamentation in its church buildings, it is possible that his two experiences with traditional Catholic architecture and sacramentality acted as a juxtaposition, creating a shock which attracted him.

Seeking God

At some point, the young adults begin to move past their initial curiosity and obstacles to becoming an active seeker of information and answers to their emerging questions about the Catholic faith. I was curious whether media had been influential with any of the participants during their search.

Internet

Four young adults indicated that they intentionally used the internet to research aspects of the Catholic faith. Notably, their search for information does not launch the spiritual journey; rather, it occurs as a secondary factor after interest is sufficiently piqued by an outside witness.

Participant D admits, "I found myself Googling 'Catholic' . . . I would just Google it when I was bored and then I downloaded music on Pandora." Similarly, Participant Q acknowledges, "I guessed it was . . . it's my responsibility to start to learn more about this instead of just going through the motions at church. So that's really when I started to pursue it a little bit more, like I started looking things up on the internet. Started watching pastors speaking online and stuff like that."

The information that Participant Q finds online, however, appears to somewhat confuse him as it conflicts with his existing religious knowledge and practice. He struggles with what he understands to be true:

> I started to research more and more about it and . . . I had like nights where I was very mad about, like, "Why it is this way?" and I had been believing in it this way. It was really hard at points to accept some things, like what I totally believed. Like at the beginning, I thought . . . like I just don't know. I was just very deterred and was like, "I don't like that." I would like to pursue that farther and then there were times . . . like no, I don't think I can ever accept that . . . like praying to the saints or praying to Mary and stuff like that. I just wondered like, "Why do I have to pray to a saint? Why can't I just pray straight to God?" And then I started to research it more, I listened more, like Father speaking online about why they do the things they do. And I started to understand it more. And once I understood it more, when I understood both sides of it.

The internet is viewed as a valuable and reliable resource not only for finding information, but also for comparison purposes. He continues,

"I won't lie, I actually typed into Google 'ten reasons why to not become a Catholic.' And I actually looked at that. I actually researched that further . . . every one of those ten reasons. But then I looked up, you know, ten reasons why to become Catholic. And they definitely conflicted. But eventually after I read numerous articles online, I made my own decision on what I believe."

One young adult used the internet to compare the beliefs of other faith traditions to discover differences in the effort to inform her individual choice. As Participant Y describes: "I have a bunch of different friends from different religions. I used to go to church with them . . . I would ask them questions about their religion. I would do some research online."

Both Participant Z and her friend, who is also attending RCIA together with her, "started to do a little more research, just about the Catholic faith and everything. And we both found it was something we wanted to pursue and see what we could do . . . mainly just Googled . . . It was like everything on the first and second page on Google. If it said 'Catholic,' that's what it was."

From a demographic perspective, it is interesting that all four participants who mentioned online research were between 21–23 years. This may suggest that "younger" young adults use technology more pervasively in their search for information. The internet may also be the initial, and even primary, medium for information.

Such a trend may raise some concern for those in parish catechesis. Without a lens through which to filter the data, young adults may not be able to adequately distinguish accurate Catholic teaching on websites. This becomes more critical due to the perceived level of truthfulness of material based on where the website ranks on key search engines such as Google.

It also puts a greater emphasis on the role of good Catholic media, which provides answers to common questions asked by young adults and in a format and language suitable to the seeker. Further, search engine optimization is critical for these sites because, as Participant Z points out, whatever weblinks rank highest on a search have a greater propensity to be clicked and subsequently skimmed and read.

Bible

Six participants indicated that they had used the Bible for informational purposes. In some cases, the participant had been exposed to Scripture during childhood yet did not express having any parental or other guidance in reading or interpreting the passages. For example, Participant Q said that her mother

> actually bought me a Children's Bible . . . It had pictures and everything . . . I couldn't grasp like the whole of the Bible itself . . . I started reading the stories of the Children's Bible and just getting a background knowledge of all that. And that really helped. Even though like I was sixteen, it just helped me, you know, start to learn about it more.

Participant Z was given a Children's Bible by a "grandmotherly" neighbor as a child. She recalls, "We called her 'granny.' She lived across the street. She was the sweetest old woman. She was always giving my brother and I books about Jesus and providing us with those. And I could never find myself to get rid of them. She also gave us a set of Children's Bibles to go through . . . so I just started going through those and learning a little bit more."

Participant X's Catholic husband bought her a Bible as a result of being unable to respond to her continual questions about the faith. She states that she immediately "started reading out of the Bible regularly."

Film and Television

Four participants indicated that they had either seen or remembered a film or television show depicting religious themes or stories. They specifically cited the films *The Ten Commandments* (1956) and *The Passion of Christ* (2004). One young adult remembered watching a cartoon series called *VeggieTales* when he was at the house of his childhood friend. However, more recent media, i.e., the contemporary PBS series *Finding Jesus* was also cited as intriguing.

Church Shopping

Five participants indicated they actively attended services of other faiths in what may be described as a kind of "church shopping." For example, Participant Y relates that "when I got out of high school, I just started going to different churches with my friends and seeing different religions." Similarly, Participant A states that she "looked at different religions that I could join."

Perhaps this level of "shopping" becomes more commonplace once the young adult becomes engaged. Both Participants P and R mention these kinds of experiences with the purpose of choosing a suitable church for their marriage ceremony. "My fiancée and I went around to a few different churches in the area, just to see what we liked," recounts Participant R.

One young adult, engaged at the time to her Catholic boyfriend, recalls, "We were looking at chapels in the area and I had a hard time with it because I didn't know anything about religion. So we went to a Baptist [church] and I walked in and it was a beautiful church but my husband was like 'nope,' 'cause he was just used to the Catholic way."

These approaches to seeking information may affirm the existence of a certain religious relativism among Christian confessions and somewhat of a religious marketplace mentality. This consumerism of religion, where young adults "stick their toe in the water," may place even greater emphasis on the first impression when one enters the parish or church environment.

Feeling "Called"

Six young adults commented on a "sense of call" they felt as their spiritual journey progressed. Both internal and external factors appear to attract the participant and motivate him or her to continue the spiritual journey. The coalescence of several factors relevant to the individual prompt him or her to make connections between experiences and draw meaning from these. Similarly, the individual may also be seeking to make sense of the series of incidences in relation to one's prior internal train of thoughts.

As an example, Participant B expresses a somewhat fatalist outlook concerning his future:

> I don't quite know how to say this . . . when we were getting ready to leave [for military service] . . . it was one of those things where it was like, it is what it is, and I know that He had a plan for me, and you know if it was going to be my time, then it was going to be my time, if it wasn't then it wasn't. Just whatever was going to be, was going to be.

After an initial meeting with the parish priest for wedding preparation, Participant E remarked, "Just meeting with Fr. _____ for that brief hour or so, you know, it definitely . . . It's just moments where you know . . . I just felt like there was something calling me."

For three of the female participants, the sense of call is strongly connected to a series of experiences or coincidences which, when aligned, are attributed to God. For Participant L, this emerges upon her reflection of several experiences which seem to her as coincidental. For example, she recalls that, immediately after a series of "deep conversations" with a close high school friend whom she describes as "very religious," she felt "goosebumps" or saw a light shining in the dark on a church or a sign as she was driving away. While she claims she does not understand God or religion at this stage, she confesses, "I felt like there was something but I didn't know what it was." Later, she connects the presence of God with her as she is going through "difficult times," such as a divorce. As she states, "I felt like I knew it was just God himself, like reaching out to me." She later relates:

> I remember I was working and something really bad happened and I had to make it to two o'clock and I didn't tell anyone at work. I just left and I was driving home and I was crying and the clouds were split with light. There was a car driving in front of me and it was driving right in front of me for a really long time. I wasn't paying attention to it and then, all of a sudden, I felt like I opened my eyes and the license plate said "blessed." And I was like "I am!" I don't know why but it was making me focus on that. And guess what? So that was in 2012. I moved to my apartment when I divorced my husband . . . I was leaving my apartment one morning and I saw that car. That person lived at my apartment. It was that license plate. It was just things that happened, they're not coincidences. Making me feel like I was at the right place at the right time. Just those kind of things have always made me feel that I needed to have a relationship with God.

She further explains:

> At the beginning of RCIA, there was a day that they handed out the Bibles and I had never had one. I had read one but I never really had one that was my own. And they were all brand new, they had never been opened. And I took mine home. And for some reason after one of the very first RCIA classes, I decided to flip through it and there was a page that was flipped down. When I opened up to that page, it had said something about children of adoption and I was adopted. I'm like immediately "oh my God," like this is pointing me to read this. Then I just felt this urge to look through my mother's belongings. My biological mom passed away from cancer in 2012. She actually had mentioned to me that she was baptized and she got a huge cross tattoo on her back. She

was trying to become more religious because she had done terrible things in her life. She was sick and I guess someone had reached her saying that God, you know, can heal things and can make you feel better as a person and forgive you for these things and stuff. So I have all of her belongings—just one bag of things—and on top of it was a Bible and I opened it. There was a piece of paper that was folded up that I had never seen before that had scriptures, like pieces of scripture . . . all these pieces of paper and the date was the exact date of that class I had, the RCIA class that I had taken in 2012. And those passages were talking about learning about faith . . . So there's just been too many things since I've started that have brought me here that have told me that this is the right thing, this is what I'm supposed to be doing.

Participant P described a particularly negative experience that her in-laws had with a local parish and contrasted this with the "welcoming" parish in which she was attending RCIA. "God knew that, so that's why he brought me there."

After Participant Z's new husband had just gone to Bahrain for his military tour of duty, she attended Mass at the parish in which she is attending RCIA. "The first service we went to, the first Mass was the day after my husband had just left for Bahrain. I was very mad at him [laughter]. So the very first Mass we went to was about forgiveness and I'm like 'Oh my God. I cannot believe this.' It was like the most mindblowing thing in the world. I was like 'wow!' I guess I'm really meant to be here today."

In some cases, the individual seems to be able to independently draw inferences, attribute meaning, or make connections to God. It is also possible that these young adults might have drawn such revelations from a healthy imagination. Gallagher notes that imagination is one of the primary means through which desire for God emerges. But he claims that imagination, like the need for belonging (which I alluded to in ch. 2), has been wounded because of the failure of recent generations to pass along the Christian faith. The impoverishment of God-images (and perhaps even self-images) has caused the individual to suffer from a kind of "amnesia or absence of roots in any tradition of meaning."[13] The wounds therefore need both healing and a stimulation of the senses in order for the nonbeliever to become more receptive toward the transcendent.

Participant D's imagination does indeed appear to have been wounded. The witness seems to train her on how to reflect on experiences and

13. Gallagher, "Woundedness and Hope," 613–30.

incidents in her life through the lens of a personal God. By keeping a journal of "blessings," she begins to make connections between what was earlier perceived as a negative event toward something that could be viewed positively.

> [The witness said] "OK, I want you to go home and I want you to write out your blessings 'cause all you think about is the sad stuff." I was like, what do you mean "my blessings"? And she's like, "I want you to just go home and write out all the good things in your life." And I'm like "okay," but what I didn't realize was that she was wanting me to sketch out all the times God saved me and all the times my mustard seeds were planted and all the times that bad things happened but good things came out. I had never looked at those things as good things for me because . . . being from my childhood all I was in the habit of was about thinking about dark, sad, depressing things, right? You get into a car accident, you're sad, but what comes out of it . . . a new car! That just happened to me so that's why I used that example.
>
> . . . She's like "you're meant to be in my life." She bought this black book like six months ago and didn't understand why. And it's perfect cause she knows I like to write. I'm a writer, like poetry, short stories, everything. We were meant to be. And she gave me this black book. It's really pretty . . . black leather and it's got old pages in it. And she writes these little spiritual messages to me. It's a little prayer for me. I'm like alright, well I guess I'll use it. And I just couldn't stop, right? I couldn't stop . . . It's like my spiritual journal . . . And she also tells me one day I'll hear God's voice but she tells me every time something happens to me or every time I come across a trial, I have to document it. So I've been doing that. So that was the second day that this all started. So I go home and . . . it's in here, my list of blessings, and I start writing down little things, like I got a cute car. And I started thinking . . . what changed my life was being adopted, and that's when I knew, not that I'm special, but that's when I knew I'm meant for something.

She later expresses from a broader scope: "So . . . my whole life is destined to become Catholic . . . it's just like everything is falling into place."

In relation to the witness, who is her professional trainer and later becomes her RCIA sponsor, she likewise attributes meaning to experiences in her life:

> Well, she wasn't supposed to be my trainer. I was supposed to have
> _____ as a trainer. His wife had gotten sick that week and so he

stepped out of work and she was replaced. And she was meant to be replaced . . . I think like that if she hadn't . . . come to me at that time, I wouldn't be . . . not that I wouldn't be here but I wouldn't be here like where I am right now. I think I am where I am right now is where I was meant to be and that's why she came into my life. (Participant D)

In this example, the believer is both literally and figuratively a "trainer," by using an abductive approach and helping Participant D to exercise her illative sense. She urges the young woman not only to notice the signs in her life, but also helps her to draw together various seemingly unconnected experiences so that she can better recognize these as the presence and guidance of God.

Fowler's Individuative-Reflective Stage

In chapter 2, I referenced James Fowler's stages of faith development. In five cases, his Individuative-Reflective stage can be observed, particularly through the participants' comments that their religious search was "one's own choice." In particular, Participant Q seems to struggle with the tension of pleasing his father and making his own decision on what he will believe. The father is concerned that the son is converting to Catholicism because of the influence of a female friend in his life.

Even though my dad questioned a lot about it, he was very supportive of it. So like no matter what decision I made, he said he was happy for me as long as it was from my heart. He didn't want me to be making a decision for someone else. So I guess that, that's definitely helpful. 'Cause I know that it would be very hard for other people, that if their parents or what not didn't accept what they were saying. Like that would cause big problems. But just because my dad was uneasy about it, it doesn't mean he didn't accept my decision. He said, you know, I'm a man now, I can make my own decisions and one day I'll be out of the house, I'll be living the life I want to, Christian or not Christian. He can't make that decision for me anymore. I think he definitely supports it now.

. . . my dad has asked me a lot about it. Like, questioned why I would make that type of decision. Everyone has kind of been asking me if it's my decision and not for her. And I've told everybody that I've talked to . . . I'd say 90 percent of it started out as like decision to do it because I wanted to but the other 10 percent was kind of, for her. But now it's like it doesn't, it doesn't really matter to me what they're thinking. I know what it is that I want. And I know that this is a decision that I want.

He likewise seems to need to prove to the RCIA director that his decision to be baptized is his own choice: "I want to show her that my faith wasn't . . . I wasn't new coming into this. Like I had thought about it for a long time . . . it was two years before I made my decision. At this point, I think it's a great decision. And it's a decision I'm not going to go back on."

After Participant K admitted that her mother and friends had been influences, she immediately emphasizes, "It was my own decision." And, despite Participant E's positive initial encounter with the parish priest during marriage preparation with his fiancée, he mentions twice that his fiancée "never really swayed me at all. Possibly she was the opening. But it was my decision, it was my choice to be in the program . . . they never really swayed me." While these comments may be indicative of the inner conflict related to finding and identifying with a faith of one's own, it is also possible they are intended to underscore the impression that one had not been pressured into attending the RCIA program.

Religion as a Life Marker

Participation in religious practices and organizations seems to be perceived as a marker for adulthood in terms of being both positively associated with and important to settling down; for young adults, this typically involves marriage, starting a new family, and raising children. Several participants acknowledged that having children, getting children baptized, or participating in the sacraments had prompted them to look more into Catholicism. Further, active participation within a community of faith may be perceived as a stabilizing factor.

For example, at the time of meeting with the parish priest for marriage preparation, Participant E realized that he wanted religion "to be more part of our lives. This is something big for us." Participant I admits, "As I'm growing older, and I don't want to say wiser, wanting to settle down, start a family, and then that aspect of my life. I really wanted to open my eyes, you know, make a commitment, make it official."

Seven participants (i.e., four male, three female) were engaged to be married at the time of making the decision to enter the RCIA process. In five of these cases, the participant's fiancé or fiancée wanted to have the marriage ceremony specifically in a Catholic church (four participants) or Christian church (one participant).

Three participants used the phrase "be on the same page," meaning that the individual felt that a common faith and practice would be beneficial to the future marriage and raising future children. None of these participants experienced a parental background which could be described as mixed faith or "no religious practice."

However, in the case where the young adult's spouse or children are already actively participating in liturgical or sacramental practices, the attraction of religion may enter more as a desire to be included and not "left out." In addition, Participant G, a married male, mentioned that he felt having the same religious faith and practicing the faith together would strengthen his existing marriage.

Eight participants spoke about the importance of knowing more about the Catholic faith out of a desire to be able to answer the questions being asked by their children. As Participant B states, his infant daughter "was getting baptized and I thought that if we were going to have her baptized and if we were going to bring her up, you know, in the Catholic faith, then I should be baptized and learn what I'm doing." Similarly, Participant N noted that she and her husband "have two kids and I was thinking about getting them baptized. And I was like, well, how can I get them to get baptized and I'm not baptized . . . it doesn't seem very fair to do that to them."

Participant C's son was already in the fourth grade in a Catholic school, which was chosen by his non-Catholic parents for its educational rather than religious value. She explains, "Around the time he was in second grade, when all of his friends were going to be doing their First Communion, he was asking me if he could get baptized and things about that nature. And, in a way I felt guilty because I didn't want to deny him that."

These insights demonstrate the importance of shallow entry points in the *ad intra* environment during the periods traditionally associated with sacramental preparation, such as baptism and first communion. The initial personal encounters with the parish should be perceived by the young adult as both welcoming and engaging. Language should be relatable and comprehensible. The clergy or parish staff member might extend an invitation to attend a small group activity.

Pre-Evangelization in the RCIA Process

The pre-catechumenate stage of the RCIA is associated with pre-evangelization and is designed to offer an opportunity for seekers to ask questions before making a formal and public commitment to continue in the study of the Catholic faith. The comments below capture insights and assess the aspects which appealed to or connected with young adults, benefits of the program, and glean implications for those in parish ministry as they relate to young adults.

For Participant N, it is not obvious how one becomes Catholic. She states, "I didn't know where to start . . . I knew that I needed to do it." Her mother-in-law acts as informant and extends an invitation for her to consider attending a local parish program. However, without the witness, the process appears to be a bit nebulous to an outsider.

For several participants in my study, as they he or she continued his or her journey through the RCIA process, the witness often remained active in the relationship and served as a means of support. In five cases, the witness was the participant's sponsor. In four additional cases, the participant was accompanied by another with whom he or she was in a close relationship (i.e., fiancé/fiancée, spouse, friend). Future or current in-laws often continued their support by attending weekly Mass with the participant and his or her fiancé or spouse.

Feeling of Trepidation

Four participants in the study specifically used the word "nervous" to describe their feeling between making the commitment to enter the RCIA and the initial meeting. This feeling seems to be connected to the feeling of being an outsider because of lack of knowledge and the fear of being negatively judged by another. As Participant O relates, "I didn't know what to expect going into it, not being from a religious upbringing. What it's going to be like. You know, like I didn't know if I was going to go in there and like 'oh, you don't know anything about this.'"

For Participant P, the sense of fear extends from her and her fiancé's initial meeting with the priest for marriage preparation to attendance at her first Mass:

> So when we came, I was so nervous and I didn't know what to say.
> I was like, "oh my gosh, we're meeting with a priest and I hope

he likes me and all of that stuff." As soon as we left, I said "this is it." . . . So we found out about the RCIA program . . . I started in September, after we got married. I waited a little bit just with all the craziness of the wedding, I wanted to be able to focus on it. We came to Mass shortly after we met with Father _____. We were sitting down and there was a child right in front of us. I was so nervous . . . I didn't know whether to stand or do what or what's happening and then, I saw the child.

Participant Q recalls experiencing the same trepidation about making the commitment to attend the RCIA, "I was a little nervous at first, because I didn't know what it was going to be about." However, he also begins to communicate these emotions with God through prayer: "I was just like 'God, just give me the words and give me the strength to make it through this and if this is what you want, then you'll make it easy for me.'"

Honoring these emotions may be important during the pre-evangelization stage. In particular, sensitivity to the individual's fears, especially the fear of being judged or pressured, may be essential on the part of both the witness and the parish staff during the time the young adult is beginning to cross the threshold from the secular to the parish environment. It is, however, encouraging and notable that each of these participants expressed that, once they began attending the RCIA program, they enjoyed going and even eagerly looked forward to the weekly gatherings.

Welcoming

Nine participants specifically used the word "welcoming" to express a positive experience in relation to the atmosphere or person(s) at the parish, either prior to or during attendance at RCIA. Other related and frequently used words included "nice" and "friendly." I probed Participant Z to inquire deeper about any individual who may have impacted her during her visit to the parish. She responded, "No one in particular 'cause everyone is incredibly welcoming and very warm, thankfully. It was just like when you came through the main door and you went into the main chapel and you sat down. You just felt at home. You felt at peace."

Participant J remarked, "I just really liked how everybody really knew each other and got along together. And really . . . it was like a family." For Participant C, the parish family becomes an extension of her local community:

> I came here, I guess you would say like through the back door. You know 'cause I was already involved with the church, but . . . second hand. Because I would do things with the school. I did things with the church and wouldn't think nothing of it, or . . . at the church Masses at the school. You know, I was here. And then we lived in the community. I mean, like I said, my neighbors belong to the church and the neighbors that don't belong to the church will still come to some of the community socials. I guess it was just moreso the sense of the community. If you have to put it in a nutshell, I guess, I would say yeah, the school, the neighborhood. Yeah, I'd say it would be the community.

Four participants specifically used the term "at home" to describe a positive sense of the parish. As Participant Y indicated, "I came here and it was like I just felt right at home." This parish experience contrasted with her experience in another religious denomination: "I sat through a couple services there. Again, but it just didn't feel at home . . . I just didn't like the atmosphere . . . I didn't really know the people. They weren't really welcoming."

The above responses indicate the importance of "belonging before believing." I use this expression as a reversal of the phrase "believing before belonging," which was coined by Grace Davie. In contrast to those who claim to be a "believer," but do not regularly attend religious services, some young adults may need to feel accepted by the parish or church community first before they will commit to participating in its services.

Flexibility

The traditional period of the RCIA runs from September or October through the liturgical feast of Pentecost, typically celebrated in late May or early June. The length of program appears to intimidate some young adults in terms of the time commitment. Participant N relates,

> It's funny because like at first when they told me [about the program], I was like, "How long is it?" Like, that was my question, right!? And they're like, "Well, we think it goes like until April." And I'm like, "April?! Well, all right." And then it actually went a little longer.

Participant D had fewer reservations about the length of the program, yet was concerned about the flexibility in relation to the process:

It was great because . . . it goes from September to Easter. And I had only . . . I want to say it was October or November . . .

Interviewer: So you started in October?

Yeah, I started late. And I'm glad I called [the parish RCIA director] because she would have had me wait.

While some participants appreciated the flexibility of the timing of RCIA program, Participant O expressed concern about the rigid structure within the program. His fears, too, seem to be allayed through the process.

I was able to take it in the way I needed to take it in. Not "you have to do this" and "this is exactly what you have to do." But it's different for everyone, you know, the way you experience it, the way you feel and stuff so . . . that was reassuring, you know . . . I didn't expect to turn into an automaton coming out but I could do it my way and feel comfortable in my way about it.

The freedom to explore one's questions and fears in a nonjudgmental environment—a "safe space"—appears to be a critical factor for young adults contemplating a change in religious belief or practice. As Participant L affirms, "I needed to have a relationship with God but I needed to be in a trusting environment where I didn't feel threatened or forced, or I didn't have to make a decision that I was uncomfortable with."

Far from being a program or rite with high entry barriers and rigid timelines, the RCIA programs at the parishes represented in this study appear to meet and adapt to where the young adult is emotionally and spiritually in the journey. The flexibility of the program respects the individuality and free will of the individual, which engenders trust.

Peers in the Parish

While perhaps not as critical in pre-evangelization, two of the participants in my study noted the importance of the presence of other young adults within the parish community as a comforting element in their journey. Perhaps the presence of others of the same age provides a kind of support and modeling of the practice of the faith. This may be a more significant factor for some young adults as they make initial contacts within the parish community.

It is also possible that young adults evaluate the strength and appeal of the parish by the demographics of the community. Questions such as:

"Do I identify with the community in terms of age? Do I look, act, and speak like the others here? Do I fit in?" may represent a kind of litmus test in terms of whether they choose to engage further with the parish or church. This does not mean an aging parish demographic will necessarily be unappealing to young adults. However if newly baptized young adults are grappling with and trying to solidify their identity as Catholics, then the local parish community may need to more actively provide support in spiritual growth rather than simply expect them to adapt to an insular style of religious practice which is reflective of a half century ago.

What Does All This Mean?

The data from this qualitative study affirmed many of the findings of previous research on young adults, which are mentioned earlier in this book. The Christian faith is not being passed down, sometimes very consciously, from parents to children. Thus, the Church now faces either a first or even second generation of "native nones," a trend that I predict will continue to grow. Young adults continue to shove off the questions related to religion or faith, sometimes because of the busyness of their lives but also because they have never been challenged to confront these questions. But negative impressions of Christianity from interactions with others can often turn off these "native nones" and away from taking the next step on the spiritual journey.

One of the most critical elements in pre-evangelization that emerges from these interviews appears to be the encounter in the secular environment with a Catholic believer. The believer acts as a witness who authentically practices the faith in a nonjudgmental manner, is unafraid to engage in conversation with the nonbeliever, is open to answering questions, and continually invites. Secondly, the method of pre-evangelization is decidedly more experiential rather than cognitive; the lifestyle and conversation of the witness are both attractive yet there is no hint of coercion to convert another. From a pastoral perspective, those involved at the parish level should be welcoming, supportive, and flexible. Thirdly, many of the young adults described in my study appear to need to "belong" before they can believe. Above all, the paradigm for pre-evangelization needs to shift from an exclusive parish-focused pre-evangelization towards a two-tier response (*ad intra* and *ad extra*) with a greater emphasis on the secular environment.

While I attempted to keep my interview questions as open-ended as possible to reduce bias, the absence of data associated with certain categories is also significant. For example, I did not find any indication of a struggle between religion and science. Nor was there any mention of the use of apologetics or an argumentative conversation in the process. None of the young adult catechumens in this study revealed a conflict with the Catholic Church, as is typically described by young adult "cradle Catholics" who have left the Church. However, it is possible that these conflicts or questions arose and were addressed during the conversations with the witness or during the RCIA program and hence were not alluded to during the interviews.

Notably, only one of the young adults expressed feelings related to a change in moral behavior. The words "sin" or "repentance" rarely enter the conversation. While this does not suggest that a focus on "sin" in the pre-evangelization stage is wrong, it may reveal that young adults do not incorporate this word in their common vocabulary, even in relation to religion or faith, or it may have a negative connotation or be associated with judgment, which is disconcerting to young adults. In some cases in this study, the young adults already utilize a language of faith. However, at the time of the interview, I estimate they likely would have been already exposed to certain pre-catechetical and catechetical material, which would have given them access to a specifically Catholic vocabulary as well as a basic foundation of theological concepts.

It is important for me to stress that the conclusions drawn from this research relate specifically to this group of young adults within a particular geographic region and cannot be applied to other young adults in another region, diocese, or confessional background within the United States. The data relates to this particular period of time, and, in a rapidly changing cultural context, some aspects of the experiences of young adults shown in this work may no longer be evident or relevant. The small sample size is inadequate to draw sweeping conclusions. While several organizations I have cited in this book have and continue to plumb the mindsets, experiences, and practices of young adults, if parishes and churches of other denominations wish to attract young adult "nones," whether native or those who have been baptized and left the pews, I believe they need to listen more closely and more deeply to these young people, rather than imposing a style of pre-evangelization which may be ineffective.

Given this data, however, we cannot remain paralyzed or stagnant in terms of how we respond. The task is not just to understand what is going on in the world of young adults, but how to change it in order that we stay true to Christ's call to mission in our parishes as well as the wider world in which we interrelate. In my final chapter, I will move toward a course of action which drives this new paradigm.

10

Where Do We Go from Here?

AFTER HAVING CONSIDERED THE contemporary worldview of young adult "native nones," examined the rationale for pre-evangelization, reflected on its various components, analyzed a contemporary model and several methods, and listened to the voices of young adults themselves, the logical question might be, "Where do we go from here?" And more specifically, "What are the implications for parishes, laypeople, and clergy?" In the field of practical theology, this final step is crucial to ensure that the lessons we have taken away from the theoretical are examined against the lived reality and then critically reflected upon. We do this with the openness to learn and change, so that appropriate action can be taken.

In this final chapter, I will synthesize the findings of the previous chapters, offering recommendations for both the *ad intra* and *ad extra* environments. Because I believe the need for pre-evangelization of young adults crosses denominational boundaries, I will also briefly address how Christians might better collaborate in a spirit of ecumenism toward the common goal of pre-evangelization. Finally, I will propose several areas for future research.

To summarize thus far, the objective of this book has been to investigate how the Catholic Church may respond to the growing number of young adults in the United States characterized as religious "native nones" in light of Jesus' call to mission. Because of a changing cultural context, I have argued that pre-evangelization may be necessary to attract these young adults and predispose them toward hearing the message of the gospel. My qualitative research affirmed many of the characteristics and trends outlined in chapter 2. Many American young adult "native nones" are unfamiliar with the teachings of the Catholic faith. This is partly due to Catholic parents neither passing down the teachings nor the practice of the faith, at times because they feel this would be an imposition on their children. While many of the participants in my study became connected with a local parish because of marriage or baptism, I detected a growing phenomenon where unchurched young adults are simply not coming to the parish on their own, even for rites of passage traditionally associated with the parish or church. Such a trend, if not reversed, will increase the population of "native nones" and result in an even greater need for pre-evangelization.

The paradigm shift in pre-evangelization, which I argue is the primary thrust of this book, moves the primary locus of this first stage from the parish to the secular world. This shift is not necessarily radical. However, I believe it puts greater onus on the laity. According to the documents of Vatican II, they are the ones who are called to be leaven in the world, to permeate and transform the culture, and be the frontline witnesses.[1]

Training for the Shift

Let us consider how this shift could impact how American clergy and laity are currently trained in evangelization. Because pre-evangelization is not well defined in ecclesial circles, diocesan religious education departments and seminaries have a vital role in helping educate those in parish leadership to understand pre-evangelization's distinction from evangelization and catechesis. Pre-evangelization does not lead with or focus on teaching the faith. This difference in emphasis implies that when young adults show up at the parish, it does not necessarily presume the young adult is ready and receptive to the *kerygma*.

Many seminarians often are required to take courses which emphasize the theology of evangelization, catechesis, and apologetics. However, the epistemological shift and movement away from apologetics as a kind of polemics suggest that the seminary curriculum might incorporate a segment on pre-evangelization as dialogue.

A practicum or field study might be helpful to expose seminarians to the hypothetical questions that unchurched young adults may have. Some

---

1. Vatican Council II, "Lumen Gentium," 30–37; Vatican Council II, "Gaudium et Spes," 43; Vatican Council II, "Apostolicam Actuositatem," 10, 18.

seminarians have already spent several years in the secular arena before responding to a potential vocation. However, after a period of intensive coursework which is highly theoretical, this practicum would allow future clergy to apply what has been read and discussed. Rather than teaching or preaching to others, it is an opportunity to be present and attentive, to not rely on preplanned or rehearsed responses. A temptation often occurs to jump into the conversation preemptively and correct the other by flooding with extensive proofs and arguments. Here, the seminarian might learn to become more sensitive to the promptings of the Holy Spirit to guide the conversation.

Given that the initial encounter in pre-evangelization will more likely take place in the secular arena, training of the laity will become more imperative. Sometimes this may be the last bullet point on the list of action items for parishes—lay witnesses may still need to be evangelized themselves! For many American Catholic parishes, the focus of existing programs is faith formation at an elementary level targeted toward current, "fallen away," or nominal Catholics. If programs include training on evangelization or sharing one's faith with others, it is typically packaged as a third tier, meaning that instruction may or may not be incorporated into the parish's curriculum.

The lack of familiarity with religious language and symbols by unchurched young adults implies that those in pre-evangelization adopt a new vocabulary which is both accessible and adjustable to its audience. The believer might avoid overly theological language which could be considered jargon, e.g., salvation, sin, hell. While the term "sin" may sound overly judgmental and indicting, an understanding of individual evil may emerge better through an awareness and discussion of social evil, such as racism or sexism. The terms "woundedness," "brokenness," or "dysfunction" may prove a better substitute to the pejorative "sin." The discussion may then lead toward one's individual responsibility toward social evil. While not negating Jesus as divine, the conversation might begin by positioning him more as a model for the human person and his teaching as a proposition for a good life. Such an approach may stimulate the possibility to learn more about Jesus, rather than merely dismiss him because of religious presumptions. Language on ethics and morality may focus on questions related to the "common good" rather than simply the individual good or a utilitarian outlook. Young adults might be prompted to consider values and meaning through questions such as: "What is important to you? What is valuable?

What is meaningful? What has given you joy?" A phrase often used by Catholic author Matthew Kelly, "becoming the best version of yourself," resonates well with the hyper-individualism of the American culture, yet still reflects the call to holiness.

At times, there is a tendency in American parishes and diocese to want to categorize and even compartmentalize young adults for the purpose of implementing a "package program." For example, Laura Niemann Anzilotti argues that dioceses and parishes operate with a "centrist" position, following a business-like approach to evangelization. [2] I suggest this centrist position demonstrates the usage of a well-organized plan through existing programming and structures. Utilizing so-called "tried and true" methods such as video series, mission talks, and book discussions can reduce some of the confusion among clergy and laity about how to evangelize others. It recognizes the local parish as the first community of outreach. However, by itself, this approach tends to become introspective and isolationist. If Catholics (and other Christians) do not move beyond the boundaries of the physical structure of their parish to engage with or encounter others, then the gospel message will be limited to a great number of young adults, especially those who have and may never step into a neighborhood church.

Hence, pre-evangelization at its best will continue to be more effective if it is approached on an individual basis and attentive to the diversity of the audience. The methods should appeal to both cognitive and experiential epistemologies. Unchurched young adults often have many questions about what the Catholic Church teaches. At times, the questions are known and can be explicitly articulated; however, questions may also be latent or buried in the subconscious and need to be coaxed out or brought to the surface. Yet young adults also have a strong desire to feel accepted without being judged. While I am not advocating a form of relativism, apologetical styles of pre-evangelization which are more deductive and polemical may be considered coercive and exclusive. Parishes may consider establishing a consistent forum or space which provides an atmosphere of freedom and openness for these questions to be expressed and explored. Similar "open space" can be carved out in the secular milieu by the witness who exhibits a willingness and welcome to respond to questions in the context of relationship.

On the other hand, young adults may more readily come to recognize aspects of the divine not through proclamation but through the experience

---

2. Anzilotti, "Evangelization," 35.

of characteristics traditionally associated with God, such as unconditional acceptance, love, forgiveness, and even suffering through a relationship with the individual witness or through the community. While American young adults may debate the existence of objective truth, an experience of genuine love and concern may not be as easily disputed. Qualities of God such as beauty or transcendence can be experienced through nature or anything deemed as mystery. Yet pre-evangelization pushes the experience a bit further by stimulating a reflection upon the experience, thereby encouraging the individual to articulate and give a language to the meaning of the experience. Hence, the young adult may inductively become familiar with the underlying themes and language of the *kerygma* before an explicit proclamation associated with evangelization.

Can I Get a Witness?

Based upon my micro-study of unbaptized young adults, the believer as witness emerges as a major element in pre-evangelization. This is consistent with teaching from magisterial documents on evangelization and other pastoral field research. In particular, the participants in my study notably described the role of the witness in terms of "antidote" and "*accompagnateur.*"

The witness serves as antidote against negative impressions or presumptions about the Catholic Church, Christianity, or Christians in general. Both authenticity and credibility remain the signposts which are becoming increasing attractive to young adults. Authenticity may provide the shock, reversal, or interruption to the young adult's unconscious or unvoiced expectations of Christians or Christianity. For example, in some cases, a reasonable, intelligent conversation may lead to the surprise or undoing of a misperception that Christians are not simple or blindly ignorant of science and can discuss a topic without resorting to scriptural proofs. The descriptor "credible" may be a rather subjective attribute depending on how it is defined by the individual. Nevertheless, credibility means that the witness seems believable to the nonbeliever.

Authenticity and credibility of the witness may imply several elements in the call to holiness, particularly for laypersons. First, a life of holiness will not consist of a veneer of piety and moral rectitude, but a humility which is aware of and admits one's individual faults and desire to overcome these through the grace of God. Out of this humility may come a willingness for a continuing renewal of attitudes and behavior, especially prejudices which may be outwardly or unconsciously projected toward the unchurched. Insomuch that holiness involves a unique and personal faithfulness to how the individual has been created, the witness becomes a testimony that a relationship with God is dynamic and multifaceted; God can call anyone and work through anyone through the immanent and ordinary. It is an antidote to a false belief that the Christian God demands a unidimensional image of followers.

The witness is also *accompagnateur*, a companion who walks with the young adult and fulfills the need for "belonging before believing." The recent *IL* document affirms the need for "spiritual paternity and maternity" and other forms of accompaniment. This may refer to the lack of role models in their native familial circumstances. [3] As the individual is considering a possible redirection of belief and lifestyle, "fitting in" becomes more relevant to the spiritual journey and an essential component of pre-evangelization. For some of the participants in my study, the sense of belonging could have emerged as a result of engagement and marriage and through acceptance by the new family. In other cases, the participant comes to feel connected with or identifies with the witness through a new or existing friendship. In the context of the parish, a healthy Christian community acts as an accompanying body, or perhaps as an earthly "cloud of witnesses," which may build upon and solidify the sense of belonging and support, especially if the young adult chooses to enter the RCIA.

Implications Ad Intra

Pre-evangelization occurs in the *ad intra* environment on three levels. The initial experience may take place when the young adult visits the parish website, physically approaches, or enters the parish environment and encounters another (who is viewed as "witness," regardless of whether this individual or persons are considered formal staff members or volunteers). Programs or events (whether cognitively or experientially based) held at the parish may be both initial or secondary experiences of encounter or conduits toward a nonbeliever's decision to attend the RCIA. Finally, a more formalized process of pre-evangelization happens during the pre-catechumenate stage in the RCIA.

Many of the narratives from participants in my study confirmed existing research on the importance of an atmosphere of welcoming, belonging,

3. *IL*, 55, 120–36.

and feeling "home" as critical and attractive characteristics which appeal to young adults. A perceived lack of engagement or hospitality was expressed by some of these participants as a factor which turned them away from a faith community. A sense of belonging and inclusion may grow if the young adult is warmly greeted in the parish entrance and verbally connects with others in the pews. During their initial parish visit, several of the young adults in my study seem to quickly evaluate or "size up" the culture and community to determine whether they seem to "fit." An initial positive experience in the parish community may stimulate the process of healing for Gallagher's "wound of belonging." Clearly, during the COVID-19 pandemic, when many parishes are either closed or offer limited opportunities for gathering, this is a great challenge. Masks make it difficult to identify newcomers. Physical distancing and fear of physical contact have suppressed the traditional norms of greeting.

As confirmed by some of the younger participants in my study, young adults may initially seek information via the internet before choosing to visit a church. Hence, the sense of welcoming may even begin with the parish website. The website represents the culture of the faith community and may often serve as the first face which young adults encounter. Graphics, content, navigation, and opportunities for interactivity can all be used to communicate and convey openness and ease of entry. Language might likewise be adjusted toward those who are seeking information at a rudimentary level.

The participants in my study confirmed that young adults value an environment where they can ask questions without fear or judgement. Parish staff might consider how to cultivate an atmosphere of trust and offer opportunities for young adults to ask questions, even before making a commitment to attend the RCIA. In a time of COVID-19, parishes might consider hosting virtual question-and-answer sessions on a regular basis for young people.

While only two young adults in my study mentioned an attraction to "mystery" in relation to the church building, the parish might seek to facilitate experiences of mystery which may be attractive to young adults. The Nightfever method is an example of how liturgy might be expressed on an "entry level" through open doors, adoration, candles, and opportunities to sit in silence. Yet at the same time, the initial encounter with the parish is a noncommittal invitation to come inside, experience, explore, and perhaps discover the unexplainable transcendent.

The insights from the HCM seem most appropriate at the level of the RCIA pre-catechumenate stage. This is the primary period when young adult "active seekers" from a variety of backgrounds and beliefs are gathered in a communal setting. Because the HCM proposes a dialogical approach to pre-evangelization, the individual responsible for organizing the RCIA sessions should be sufficiently grounded in broad possibilities for dialogue without falling into a didactic style which focuses on mere transmission of church doctrine. If, according to the HCM, both clergy and laity are expected to be experts and "specialists," then education and formation programs may need to incorporate more material on other religions (including atheism) so there is a basic familiarity with these, together with possible language used by young adults when conversing on religion or spirituality. An ignorance of other perspectives may cause the individual to lapse into deductive mentality, which becomes more defensive than explorative.

Feedback from my study indicates that those in pastoral ministry may wish to reconsider the length of time dedicated to the pre-catechumenate, a period which is formally designed for the pre-evangelization stage associated with inquiry.[4] A more flexible period of time will allow young adults to ask questions and explore their own understanding of the Catholic faith without a definitive limit in which they need to proceed to the subsequent stage of the catechumenate. There is, I believe, a much greater difference between the pre-catechumenate stage and the catechumenate stage in terms of approach, where individuals are able to and willing to receive formal instruction in the Catholic faith.

If a lengthier pre-catechumenate is advocated, then clergy and pastoral workers may rightly raise the question of when the gospel message is most appropriately introduced in the RCIA process. In addition, at what point does the pastoral staff extend the invitation to the young adult seeker to continue further? This decision requires a level of sensitivity as well as being attuned to the indications of when the young adult may wish to deepen his or her understanding. At the least, the movement into the catechumenate should be by invitation rather than a prescribed and predetermined time.

I wish to stress that pre-evangelization does not negate the need for the New Evangelization. Many of the parents of the young adult participants in my study might be considered the exact audience for this

---

4 In *CIC*, c. 788.1–3, the length of the pre-catechumenate period is not specifically defined, only that those "who have manifested a willingness to embrace faith in Christ are to be admitted to the catechumenate."

outreach. These "former" or "fallen away" Catholics need to rediscover the beauty of their native faith and even experience a first encounter with Jesus Christ. Similarly, those young adults who have been baptized in the Catholic Church but never evangelized may likewise need a so-called fresh start or reboot to stimulate the seed of faith received sacramentally by grace. Certainly, some aspects of pre-evangelization could apply to the New Evangelization. For example, parish staff and believers in the *ad extra* environment need to take time to listen to why individuals have chosen to leave the Church. Are there presuppositions or erroneous understandings? Is there a negative emotional component associated with an event that one has experienced within the Church?

Implications Ad Extra

The narratives in chapter 9 overwhelmingly support the critical role of a credible and authentic witness in pre-evangelization outside of the parish walls. In contrast to a parish setting where the young adult might interact with multiple individuals, the encounter in the secular milieu appears to be more one-on-one.

Given this situation, the HCM should be adapted toward a more individualized encounter. I have already provided several suggestions in chapter 7. The believer as witness acts more as a representative of Christ, imperfect, on his or her own faith journey. He or she may not have all the answers to the questions. In several cases in my study, the believer seems to challenge the young adult to seek more information through outside material. Because young adults are increasingly turning to electronic resources, parishes might disseminate links of orthodox and compelling websites, blogs, and videos which can be accessed at leisure.

The observation of an increasing curiosity and greater number of questions might be a logical prompt during the pre-evangelization process where the believer can gently invite the young adult to take the next step to investigate the RCIA. Other faith denominations have their own formal or programmatic responses to this stage of evangelization or catechesis.

In Geisler's conversational method, the encounter with the witness may appear to be more of an orchestrated or manipulated event. While this approach might be traditionally associated with certain intentional styles of evangelism or pre-evangelism, the experience of surprise or shock associated with pre-evangelization supports more of a random meeting, while insisting that the believer remain open and receptive to its occurrence. However, the building of relationships which engender the level of trust without appearing to be unidimensional toward conversion may imply a much longer process and hence, greater patience. Pre-evangelization becomes less expedient or utilitarian in terms of reaching the goal of proclaiming the *kerygma* and instead becomes more relational.

None of the participants in my study described encountering a priest outside of the parish setting. This does not mean that parish-based clergy have no role to play in pre-evangelization, but it may imply that pre-evangelization *ad extra* may be considered a bit of unchartered territory. This raises several questions, all of which could serve as suitable prompts for pre-evangelization: (1) How often do pastors venture outside the parish to encounter young adults in commonly frequented secular locations, such as bars, restaurants, or sports events? (2) Do priests wear clerical clothing which identifies them as Catholic priests or do they wear clothing typically associated with the laity? Is this a benefit or a liability for pre-evangelization? (3) Will young adults be more or less open to approach or be approached by a Catholic priest based upon their outward appearance?

The encounter with transcendence need not occur in traditional sacred places, such as those associated with institutional religion or faith, but can take place in the immanence of daily life. Several participants in my study communicated a sense of awe, mystery, and transcendence which they discovered during a period of silence, the beauty of nature, and even through the birth of a child. Not all young adults will link transcendence with these natural phenomena and may indeed demonstrate a certain apathy or incredulity; in these circumstances, the believer may act as a catalyst to prompt questions, with the goal of stimulating reflection upon the experience rather than dismissing it. Further, the believer can provide a new lens of interpretation of experiences by asking the young adult to recall and relate previous experiences in which they felt particularly moved and connecting these to find meaning, hence developing and strengthening the illative sense. Exercising Newman's illative sense does not depend upon the collection of and reflection of facts; if contemporary young adults substitute experiences for facts as an epistemological base or preference for discovering information, then reflection upon previous experiences and the emotions connected may help to de-atomize the experiences and draw out connections and meaning to these events.

Finally, if evangelization is viewed through the lens of St. Paul's image of a spiritual battle, using military terms I propose that the laity who seek to pre-evangelize in the realm of the *ad extra* may be termed less as "frontline soldiers" (Eph 6:10–20)[5] whether in an offensive or defensive role and instead function more as scouts. They do not forge ahead blindly with a kerygmatic message that is coercive. Likewise, they do not approach or encounter the nonbeliever with a self-effacing or even prideful and argumentative defense of Christianity. Rather, they move forward into unknown territory, seeking to better understand the inhabitants, how they think and react, what they know and do not. They adjust their tactics according to the scene. A scout will duly inform those "generals" and others in ecclesial administrative roles so that both theory and practice of pre-evangelization are consistent with the signs of the times.

Implications for Ecumenism

In chapter 8, I examined several perspectives and methods of pre-evangelization (or pre-evangelism) from Catholic as well as various Protestant confessional backgrounds. Many of the methods (e.g., Alpha, L'Abri, Taizé) could be considered ecumenical in terms of collaboration and outreach; while their theology is faithful to their founders, the intended audience crosses confessional boundaries. Yet, there is still a lack of agreement on the scriptural validity and methods of pre-evangelism. While outside the scope of this book, I acknowledge the epistemological foundations related to soteriology and the nature of grace which have contributed to diversity in confessional beliefs toward pre-evangelization. With respect to future ecumenical activity, these differences should not be naively dismissed or glossed over.

A more inclusive definition of ecumenism, which incorporates activities and initiatives of both clergy and laity, would promote mutual understanding and unity among all Christians. I would challenge continued dialogue among Catholics, Orthodox, and Protestants to recognize diversity with regards to the methods in which pre-evangelization takes place in accordance with new ways and languages according to the audience. This foundation has already been laid among Protestant denominations since Edinburgh's International Missionary Conference in the early 1900s and through the World Council of Churches (WCC) out of a mutual concern

5. According to Vatican Council II, "Apostolicam Actuositatem," 38, laypersons are considered "on the front lines" in evangelization.

and support for mission. Christians have agreed on the need to spread the gospel, albeit there remains disagreement on how this "good news" is both revealed and manifested. These efforts have also brought about an evolution or broadening of the understanding of mission beyond proclamation. This may affirm the WCC decision that evangelism is part of the wider *missio dei*, but not exclusively the *missio dei*. Perhaps if this mission can be understood more as "witness without explicit proclamation," allowing for a later "witness with proclamation," then there can be greater common ground among denominations for pre-evangelization.

In cooperative or "grass-roots" ecumenism, the laity act as the primary agents. Their focus is not on resolving theological disagreements or trying to achieve structural unity; instead, they seek to take what they already have in common as the basis for doing something together.[6] I sought to draw attention to the importance of the laity in pre-evangelization efforts *ad extra*, ecumenical work and activity seems to be most crucial on an immediate timeframe. The American Church is already in the middle of a faith crisis for young adults which begs most stridently for an ecumenical response and exploration for a future collaboration in efforts toward pre-evangelization. Catholics and Protestants (and Orthodox, for that matter) are facing the same dearth of membership and loss of its young people in the pews and share the same concern for the growing atheism, secularization, and materialism which affect youth and young adults.

Ecumenical dialogue in pre-evangelization recognizes that we can all learn from one another, to discern and appreciate the good in each other's methods, and move toward more of an "exchange of gifts" rather than a retreat into denominational silos.[7] Perhaps a goal at both the dialogical and cooperative levels would be to strive for unity in purpose without regressing to polemics over uniformity in method. After all, does not the goal of inculturation of the gospel with a personalist approach necessitate diversity?

Recommendations for Further Research

Admittedly, there are many topics connected to pre-evangelization which could be explored in greater depth. More research could be conducted with a broader demographic audience to take advantage of a wider number of experiences. Further, by isolating some of the factors such as geography,

6. Kinzer, "Cooperative Ecumenism."

7. Vatican Council II, "Unitatis Redintegratio," 28–29.

socio-economic levels, ethnicity, and perhaps even young adults in detention facilities, different aspects on pre-evangelization might surface and new implications be gleaned.

This study began with statistical data on American young adult "nones," a term which encompasses a wide swath of spirituality and religious beliefs. However, none of the young adults in my sample self-identified as agnostic or atheist. Isolating these factors may provide more varied information on how pre-conversion experiences differ from those of the young adults with a liminal religious background. A possible study could be done on the blogs describing young adults' conversions to Catholicism. Alternative approaches and methods of pre-evangelization might emerge or predominate in these cases.

While I did not interview the witnesses of the young adults in my study, the role of the witness could be explored in greater depth. More research could be undertaken to determine the witnesses' religious or spiritual backgrounds, education, as well as their confidence levels in discussing various aspects of spiritualty or religious beliefs or responding to questions about the Catholic faith. For example, how does the witness see herself or himself in the role? Did he/she feel adequately prepared for the task? If so, what was the background or education level? This feedback would shed light on further avenues for education and formation of the laity.

The theme of welcoming emerged strongly from this study. Another interesting line of research would be to analyze the parish environment in urban, suburban, and rural locations. An observational study might be made on the physical layout of the parish. Is there sufficient space to gather? How do religious symbols in the physical space impact a sense of welcome or even judgement? Young adults might be probed for information on their initial visits to parishes for the purpose of investigating, for example, perceived hospitality, response to the parish audience, and likelihood to return. Parish staff and parishioners could also be queried to uncover how they view their role in welcoming newcomers.

The world in which American young adults connect with information and other individuals is rapidly changing in terms of technology. While I believe there are a growing number of opportunities to use new media to reach this audience, I also believe that this venue is still in its infancy. A possible line of research would be to explore the usage of websites and blogs specifically directed toward unchurched young adults. How have young adults engaged in various new media and how it has affected them in terms of their response to faith? Alternatively, are there overall themes or questions which emerge from these forums and how do those who manage websites and blogs respond?

Concluding Comments

As I draw this book to a close, I am often asked in ecclesial circles for a series of prescriptions on how to attract young adults to the Catholic Church. While I am not abdicating or avoiding the question, conversion in all its stages is highly complex and thus requires individualization of response. The stories of the twenty-four young adults have confirmed that I cannot concretize or even McDonald-ize even this earliest stage of conversion. Clearly, there are many more aspects and tangents related to pre-evangelization, which need to be investigated; I have only mentioned a few of these possible avenues in this chapter. My hope is that this book will become a platform for further future discussion and collaboration among Christian denominations on this topic. I believe this not only affirms Christ's call to "make disciples" but also that we "all may be one."

Appendix

Demographic Characteristics of Participants in Qualitative Study

Participant	Age (years)	Gender	Ethnicity	Education	Marital Status
A	25	Female	White	Bachelor Degree	Single
B	33	Male	Latino/ Hispanic	Some College	Married
C	31	Female	Black	Bachelor Degree	Married
D	23	Female	Black	Some College	Single
E	28	Male	White	Bachelor Degree	Single
F	33	Male	White	Some College	Married
G	29	Male	White	Bachelor Degree	Single
I	24	Female	White	Associate Degree	Married
J	24	Female	Asian	Bachelor Degree	Single
K	27	Female	White	Master Degree	Married
L	35	Female	White	Bachelor Degree	Married
M	36	Female	White	Bachelor Degree	Married
N	28	Male	White	Associate Degree	Single
O	27	Female	White	Bachelor Degree	Married
P	21	Male	White	Some College	Single

Participant	Age (years)	Gender	Ethnicity	Education	Marital Status
Q	24	Male	White	Bachelor Degree	Single
R	35	Female	White	College Certificate	Married
S	30	Female	White	Bachelor Degree	Married
T	25	Female	White	Bachelor Degree	Single
U	20	Female	White	Some College	Single
V	26	Female	White	College Certificate	Married
W	29	Female	White	Some College	Married
X	23	Female	White	Some High School	Single
Y	22	Female	White	High School Diploma	Married
Z	25	Female	White	Bachelor Degree	Single

NOTE: Data on Participant H was later discarded because of status as RCIA candidate (i.e., participant had been baptized into another Christian faith).

Some College: A high school diploma or the equivalent, plus the completion of one or more postsecondary courses that did not result in any degree or award.

College Certificate: Award (but not a degree) given for attainment of a defined occupational program, often vocational.

Bibliography

Abraham, William. *The Logic of Evangelism*. Grand Rapids: Eerdmans, 1996.

Adams, Daniel J. "Toward a Theological Understanding of Post-Modernism." *CrossCurrents* 47, no. 4 (Winter 1997/1998) 518–30.

Allen, John. "Francis and the 'Culture of Encounter.'" *National Catholic Reporter*, December 20, 2013. https://www.ncronline.org/blogs/ncr-today/francis-and-culture -encounter.

Anderson, Leith. *A Church for the 21st Century*. Bloomington, MN: Bethany, 1992.

Anzilotti, Laura N. "Evangelization: Three Contemporary Approaches." In *Evangelizing America*, edited by Thomas Rausch, 28–49. Mahwah, NJ: Paulist, 2004.

Aquinas, Thomas. *Summa Theologica*. 3 vols. Translated by Fathers of the English Dominican Province. London: Burns, Oates & Washbourne Ltd., 1922.

Arnett, Jeffrey. *Emerging Adulthood: The Winding Road from the Late Teens through the Twenties*. New York: Oxford University Press, 2004.

Barna Group. "Almost Half of Practicing Christian Millennials Say Evangelism Is Wrong." February 5, 2019. https://www.barna.com/research/millennials-oppose-evangelism/.

———. "David Kinnaman and Jon Tyson Discuss Millennials, 'Nones', and a Renewed Vision for Church." April 1, 2014. https://www.barna.com/research/david-kinnaman-and-jon-tyson-discuss-millennials-nones-and-a-renewed-vision-for-church/.

———. *Making Space for Millennials: A Blueprint for Your Culture, Ministry, Leadership and Facilities*. Ventura, CA: Barna Group, 2015.

———. "Millennials and the Bible: 3 Surprising Insights." October 21, 2014. https://www.barna.com/research/millennials-and-the-bible-3-surprising-insights/.

———. "What Americans Think of Pope Francis and His Policies." September 16, 2015. https://www.barna.com/research/what-americans-think-of-pope-francis-and-his-policies/.

Barth, Karl. "The Awakening to Conversion." In *The Doctrine of Reconciliation*, edited by G. W. Bromiley and T. F. Torrance, 173–205. Vol. 4.2 of *Church Dogmatics*. Edinburgh: T&T Clark, 1938.

———. *The Doctrine of Reconciliation*. Vol. 4.2 of *Church Dogmatics*. Edinburgh: T&T Clark, 1938.

Beaudoin, Tom. *Virtual Faith: The Irreverent Quest of Generation X*. San Francisco: Jossey-Bass, 1998.

Bellah, Robert, ed. *Habits of the Heart: Individualism and Commitment in American Life*. Berkeley: University of California Press, 1985.

Benedict XVI. "Address to the Members of the Episcopal Conference of Portugal on Their 'Ad Limina' Visit." November 10, 2007. Vatican.va.

———. *General Audience: St. Paul's "Conversion"*. September 3, 2008. Vatican.va.

———. *New Technologies, New Relationships. Promoting a Culture of Respect, Dialogue and Friendship*. May 24, 2009. Vatican.va.

Bergoglio, Jorge. "For Man." In *A Generative Thought: An Introduction to the Works of Luigi Giussani*, edited by Elisa Buzzi, 79–83. Montreal: McGill-Queens University Press, 2003.

Bloesch, Donald. *A Theology of Word and Spirit: Authority and Method in Theology*. Downers Grove: InterVarsity, 2005.

———. *Theological Notebook*. Vol. 3, *1969–1983: The Spiritual Journals of Donald Bloesch*. Eugene, OR: Wipf and Stock, 2005.

Bobkowski, Piotr S., and Lisa D. Pearce. "Baring Their Souls in Online Profiles or Not? Religious Self-disclosure in Social Media." *Journal for the Scientific Study of Religion* 50 (December 2011) 744–62.

Booker, Mike, and Mark Ireland. *Evangelism—Which Way Now? An Evaluation of Alpha, Emmaus, Cell Church and Other Contemporary Strategies for Evangelism*. London: Church House, 2010.

Buber, Martin. *Ich und Du (I and Thou)*. Translated by Ronald Gregor Smith. Edinburgh: T&T Clark, 1937.

Buechsel, Tim. "One Size Fits All? Uncovering Multiple Conversion Avenues for Effective Evangelism." DMin diss., George Fox University, 2013.

Buzzi, Elisa, ed. *A Generative Thought: An Introduction to the Works of Luigi Giussani*. Montreal: McGill-Queens University Press, 2003.

"Cardinal Ratzinger Commends U.S. Model of Laicism." *Zenit*, November 25, 2004. https://zenit.org/articles/cardinal-ratzinger-commends-u-s-model-of-laicism/.

Casti, Manuela. "Taizé: A Case Study." PhD diss., Kings College London, 2015.

Code of Canon Law: Latin-English Edition. Washington, DC: Canon Law Society of America, 1999.

Congregation for the Clergy. *General Directory for Catechesis*. Washington, DC: USCCB, 1998.

Cowan, Steven B., ed. *Five Views on Apologetics*. Grand Rapids: Zondervan, 2000.

Crotty, Michael. *The Foundations of Social Research: Meaning and Perspective in the Research Process*. 2nd ed. London: Sage, 1998.

Davie, Grace. "Is Europe an Exceptional Case?" *The Hedgehog Review* (Spring/Summer 2006) 23–34.

Dawson, Christopher. *Understanding Europe*. London: Sheed and Ward, 1952.

De las Casas, Bartolomé. *History of the Indies*. Translated and edited by Andrée Collard. New York: Harper & Row, 1971.

Derrida, Jacques. *Of Grammatology.* Translated by Gayatri Chakravorty Spivak. Baltimore: Johns Hopkins University Press, 1967.

Dillen, Annemie, and Didier Pollefeyt. "Catechesis Inside Out: A Hermeneutical Model for Catechesis in Parishes." *The Person and the Challenges* 1 (2011) 151–77.

Dulles, Avery. *Evangelization for the Third Millennium.* Mahwah, NJ: Paulist, 2009.

———. "The Impact of the Catholic Church on American Culture." In *Evangelizing America*, edited by Thomas Rausch, 11–26. Mahwah, NJ: Paulist, 2004.

———. "John Paul II and the New Evangelization: What Does It Mean?" In *John Paul II and the New Evangelization*, edited by Ralph Martin and Peter Williamson, 2–16. Cincinnati: Servant, 2006.

Durkheim, Emile. *The Elementary Forms of Religious Life.* New York: George Allen & Unwin Ltd., 1915.

"Establishment Clause." Cornell Law School, Legal Information Institute, n.d. https://www.law.cornell.edu/wex/establishment_clause.

"Five Trends Among the Unchurched." Barna Group, October 9, 2014. https://www.barna.com/research/five-trends-among-the-unchurched/.

Ford, Leighton. *The Power of Story: Discovering the Oldest, Most Natural Way to Reach People for Christ.* Colorado Springs, CO: NavPress, 1995.

Foucault, Michel. *Power/Knowledge: Selected Interviews and Other Writings, 1972–1977.* Edited by Colin Gordon. New York: Random House, 1980.

Fowler, James W. *Stages of Faith: The Psychology of Human Development and the Quest for Meaning.* San Francisco: Harper, 1981.

Francis I. *Christus Vivit. Evangelii Gaudium.* Frederick, MD: The Word Among Us, 2013.

———. *Lumen Fidei.* June 29, 2013. Vatican.va.

Gallagher, Michael Paul. "Christian Identity, A Perspective from Lonergan." In *Christian Identity in a Postmodern Age: Celebrating the Legacies of Karl Rahner and Bernard Lonergan*, edited by Declan Marmion, 143–61. Dublin: Veritas, 2005.

———."Woundedness and Hope for Faith Today." *Studia Patavina* 51 (2004) 613–30.

Gecewicz, Claire. "U.S. Catholics, Non-Catholics Continue to View Pope Francis Favorably." Pew Research Center. January 18, 2017. http://www.pewresearch.org/fact-tank/2017/01/18/favorable-u-s-views-pope-francis/.

Geisler, Norman, and David Geisler. *Conversational Evangelism: How to Listen and Speak So You Can be Heard.* Eugene, OR: Harvest, 2009.

Giussani, Luigi. *At the Origin of the Christian Claim.* Montreal: McGill-Queens University Press, 1998.

———. *The Journey to Truth Is an Experience.* Montreal: McGill-Queens University Press, 2006.

———. *Morality: Memory and Desire.* Translated by K.D. Whitehead. San Francisco: Ignatius, 1986.

———. *The Religious Sense.* Montreal: McGill-Queens University Press, 1997.

Gorski, John F. "From 'Mission' to 'New Evangelization': The Origins of a Challenging Concept." Lecture, Missionary Societies of Apostolic Life Meeting, Maryknoll, NY, October 27, 2011.

Gray, Mark M., and Paul M. Perl. *Sacraments Today: Belief and Practices Among U.S. Catholics.* Washington, DC: Center for Applied Research in the Apostolate, 2008.

Greer, Robert. *Mapping Postmodernism: A Survey of Christian Options.* Downers Grove: InterVarsity, 2003.

Griffin, David Ray, et al. *Varieties of Postmodern Theology.* Albany: State University of New York Press, 1989.

Guardini, Romano, and Heinz R. Kuehn. *The Essential Guardini.* Chicago: Liturgy Training, 1997.

Halbach, Matt. "New Pope, New Evangelization, New Return to Old (but Good) Ideas." *Catechetical Leader* 24 (September 2013) 17–21.

Heard, James. *Inside Alpha: Explorations in Evangelism.* Eugene, OR: Wipf and Stock, 2012.

Hervieu-Léger, Danièle. *Religion as a Chain of Memory.* New Brunswick, NJ: Rutgers University Press, 2000.

Hill, Bradley N. "Missing the Signs: The Church and Gen Y." *Christian Century* 128 (April 5, 2011). https://www.christiancentury.org/article/2011-03/missing-signs.

Hill, Brennan R. *The Ongoing Renewal of Catholicism.* Winona, MN: Saint Mary's, 2008.

Hirsch, Alan. *The Forgotten Ways: Reactivating the Missional Church.* Grand Rapids: Brazos, 2006.

Hoffman, Louis, and Marika Kurzenberger. "Premodern, Modern, and Postmodern Interpretations of the Miraculous and Mental Illness from Religious and Psychological Perspectives." In *Parapsychological Perspectives*, edited by J. Harold Ellens, 65–93. Vol. 3 of *Miracles: God, Science, and Psychology in the Paranormal.* Westport, CT: Praeger, 2008.

Hofinger, Johannes, and Francis J. Buckley. *The Good News and Its Proclamation: Post-Vatican II Edition of The Art of Teaching Christian Doctrine.* Notre Dame: University of Notre Dame Press, 1968.

Hofinger, Johannes, and Theodore Stone, eds. *Pastoral Catechetics.* New York: Herder and Herder, 1964.

Hoge, Dean R., et al. *Young Adult Catholics: Religion in the Culture of Choice.* Notre Dame: University of Notre Dame Press, 2001.

Hostetler, Bob. "Who Changed the Cultural Channel? How a Basic Understanding of Postmodernism Can Make Your Ministry More Effective." *Discipleship Journal* 22 (May/June 2002).

John Paul II. *Catechesi Tradendae.* October 16, 1979. Vatican.va.

———. *Ecclesia in America.* January 22, 1999. Vatican.va.

———. *Redemptoris Missio.* December 7, 1990. Vatican.va.

Jungmann, Josef Andreas. *Die Frohbotschaft und unsere Glaubensverkundigung.* Regensburg: Verlag Friedrich Pustet, 1936.

———. *Pastoral Liturgy.* New York: Herder and Herder, 1962.

Kimball, Dan. *They Like Jesus but Not the Church: Insights from Emerging Generations.* Grand Rapids: Zondervan, 2007.

Kinnaman, David. *You Lost Me: Why Young Christians Are Leaving the Church . . . And Rethinking Faith.* Grand Rapids: Baker, 2011.

Kinnaman, David, and Gabe Lyons. *unChristian: What a New Generation Really Thinks about Christianity . . . and Why It Matters.* Grand Rapids: Baker, 2007.

Kinzer, Mark S. "Cooperative Ecumenism: Being Different Without Being Distant." *Living Bulwark* 94 (October/November 2017). http://www.swordofthespirit.net/bulwark/october2017p4.htm.

Klemm, David E., and William H. Klink. "Constructing and Testing Theological Models." *Zygon* 38 (2003) 495–528.

Kosmin, Barry A. "American Secular Identity, Twenty-First-Century Style: Secular College Students in 2013." *Free Inquiry* 34 (June/July 2014). https://secularhumanism. org/2014/05/cont-american-secular-identity-twenty-first-century-style-secular-college-s/.

Kosmin, Barry A., and Ariela Keysar. *American Religious Identification Survey 2008 Summary Report.* Hartford, CT: Institute for the Study of Secularism in Society & Culture, 2009.

Kosmin, Barry A., et al. *American Religious Identification Survey.* Hartford, CT: Trinity College, 2001.

Kramer, Rachelle. "Filling the Spiritual Void: Liturgical Prayer that Nourishes Catholic Millennials." *Obsculta* 6 (2013) 43–51.

Kuhn, Thomas. *The Structure of Scientific Revolutions.* 2nd ed. Chicago: University of Chicago Press, 1970.

Leggett, Tabatha. "Inside Alpha: An Atheist's Foray Into Christianity." *New Statesman*, June 20, 2013. https://www.newstatesman.com/religion/2013/06/inside-alpha-atheists-foray-christianity.

Lemna, Keith, and David Delaney. "Three Pathways into the Theological Mind of Pope Francis." *Nova et Vetera* 12 (2014) 25–56.

Liègè, Pierre-André. "Evangelization." *Catholicisme IV* (1956) 756–64.

Lipset, Seymour Martin. *Continental Divide: The Values and Institutions of the United States and Canada.* New York: Routledge, 1990.

Lombaerts, Herman, and Didier Pollefeyt. "The Emergence of Hermeneutics in Religious Education Theories." In *Hermeneutics and Religious Education*, edited by Herman Lombaerts and Didier Pollefeyt, 3–53. Leuven: Leuven University Press, 2004.

Lyotard, Jean-Francois. *The Postmodern Condition: A Report on Knowledge.* Translated by Geoff Bennington and Brian Massumi. Minneapolis: University of Minnesota Press, 1979.

Mabry, John R. *Faithful Generations: Effective Ministry Across Generational Lines.* New York: Morehouse, 2013.

Machen, J. Gresham. "Christianity and Culture." *The Princeton Theological Review* 11 (1913) 1–15.

Mathewes, Charles T. "Interview with Peter Berger." *The Hedgehog Review* 8, no. 1–2 (Spring/Summer 2006) 152–62.

McBrien, Richard. *Catholicism.* San Francisco: HarperCollins, 1994.

McGrath, Alister. *Mere Apologetics: How to Help Seekers & Skeptics Find Faith.* Grand Rapids: Baker, 2012.

McKinney, Rick D. "Using Storytelling (Including Image, Metaphor, and Narrative) in Cross-Generational and Cross-Cultural Twenty-First Century Evangelism." DMin diss., George Fox University, 2014.

McManis, Clifford B. *Biblical Apologetics: Advancing and Defending the Gospel of Christ.* Bloomington, IN: Xlibris Corporation, 2012.

Mercadante, Frank. *Engaging a New Generation: A Vision for Reaching Catholic Teens.* Huntington, IN: Our Sunday Visitor, 2012.

Mercadante, Linda. "The Seeker Next Door: What Drives the Spiritual but Not Religious?" *Christian Century* 129.11 (2012) 30–33.

Mitchell, Kathleen. "Are They Finding a Place in Our Parishes? Young Adult Catholics and the New Evangelization." *New Theology Review* 26 (September 2013) 75–78.

Molloy, Connor. "Four Things That Keep Millennials from Finding God, according to Fr. Robert Spitzer." *Catholic World Report*, February 29, 2016. http://www.catholicworldreport.com/Item/4615/the_four_things_keeping_millennials_from_finding_god_according_to_fr_spitzer.aspx.

Mongoven, Anne Marie. *The Prophetic Spirit of Catechesis: How We Share the Fire in Our Hearts*. Mahwah, NJ: Paulist, 2000.

Muldoon, Tim. *Seeds of Hope: Young Adults and the Catholic Church in the United States*. Mahwah, NJ: Paulist, 2008.

Nebreda, Alfonso. "East Asian Study Week on Mission Catechetics." *Lumen Vitae* 17 (1962) 717–30.

———. *Kerygma in Crisis?*. Chicago: Loyola University Press, 1965.

———. "The Mission of the Society in a Dechristianized World." *The Way Supplement* 20 (1973) 94–104.

Newman, John Henry. *Essay in Aid of a Grammar of Assent*. New York: Longmans, Green, and Co., 1906.

Newman, Randy. "Leveling the Playing Field: A Strategy for Pre-Evangelism." *Knowing & Doing* (Winter 2015) 1–3.

———. *Questioning Evangelism: Engaging People's Hearts the Way Jesus Did*. Grand Rapids: Kregel, 2002.

Pathrapankal, Joseph. *Time and History: Biblical Theological Studies*. Eugene, OR: Wipf and Stock, 2005.

Paul VI. *Evangelii Nuntiandi*. December 8, 1975. Vatican.va.

Pew Research Center. "America's Changing Religious Landscape." *Religion and Public Life*, May 12, 2015. http://www.pewforum.org/2015/05/12/americas-changing-religious-landscape/.

———. "Faith in Flux: Changes in Religious Affiliation in the U.S." *Religion and Public Life*, April 27, 2009. http://www.pewforum.org/2009/04/27/faith-in-flux/.

———. Millennials: A Portrait of Generation Next: Confident, Connected, Open to Change." February 2010. http://pewsocialtrends.org/assets/pdf/millennials-confident-connected-open-to-change.pdf.

———. "Millennials in Adulthood: Detached from Institutions, Networked with Friends." *Social and Demographic Trends*, March 7, 2014. http://www.pewsocialtrends.org/2014/03/07/millennials-in-adulthood/.

———. "Nones on the Rise: One-in-Five Adults Have No Religious Affiliation." *Religion and Public Life*, October 9, 2012. https://www.pewresearch.org/wp-content/uploads/sites/7/2012/10/NonesOnTheRise-full.pdf.

———. "Social Media Use in 2018." *Internet and Technology*, March 1, 2018. http://www.pewinternet.org/2018/03/01/social-media-use-in-2018.

———. "U.S. Religious Knowledge Survey." *Religion and Public Life*, September 28, 2010. http://www.pewforum.org/2010/09/28/u-s-religious-knowledge-survey/.

———. "U.S. Religious Landscape Survey: Religious Beliefs and Practices." *Religion and Public Life*, June 1, 2008. http://www.pewforum.org/2008/06/01/u-s-religious-landscape-survey-religious-beliefs-and-practices/.

Phan, Peter. "Evangelizationin a Culture of Pluralism: Challenges and Opportunities." *Australian eJournal of Theology* 9, no. 1 (March 2007) 1–15.

Pollefeyt, Didier. *Class Notes: Course Didactics (A0950) Religious Education*. Leuven: Centre for Academic Teacher Training, 2012.

————. "Difference Matters: A Hermeneutic-Communicative Concept of Didactics of Religion in a European Multi-Religious Context." *Journal of Religious Education* 56 (2008) 9–17.

————. "Hermeneutical-Communicative Religious Education in a Nutshell." *Catechetische Service* 34 (2007) 14–16.

————. *Reader: Course Didactics (A0950) Religious Education.* Leuven: Centre for Academic Teacher Training, 2012.

Prothero, Stephen. *God Is Not One: The Eight Rival Religions that Rule the World.* New York: HarperOne, 2011.

————. *Religious Literacy: What Every American Needs to Know—And Doesn't.* San Francisco: HarperCollins, 2007.

Rambo, Lewis R. *Understanding Religious Conversion.* New Haven, CT: Yale University Press, 1993.

Reed, Randy. "A Book for None? Teaching Biblical Studies to Millennial Nones." *Teaching Theology & Religion* 19 (April 2016) 154–74.

Rorty, Richard. *Consequences of Pragmatism: Essays, 1972–1980.* Minneapolis: University of Minnesota Press, 1982.

Rymarz, Richard. "Principles of the New Evangelization: Analysis and Direction." PhD diss., Australian Catholic University, 2010.

Santos, Jason Brian. *A Community Called Taizé: A Story of Prayer, Worship, and Reconciliation.* Downers Grove: InterVarsity, 2008.

Savarona, Alberto. *The Life of Luigi Giussani.* Translated by Mariangela C. Sullivan and Christopher Bacich. Montreal: McGill-Queen's University Press, 2018.

Schaeffer, Francis. *Art and the Bible.* Downers Grove: InterVarsity, 1973.

————. *The Complete Works of Francis A. Schaeffer: A Christian Worldview.* 5 vols. Westchester, IL: Crossway, 1982.

Scharlemann, Robert. "Theological Models and Their Construction." *Journal of Religion* 53 (January 1973) 65–82.

Schneider, Matthew P. "Applying Six Offline Models to Online Evangelization." *Homiletics and Pastoral Review,* June 28, 2017. http://www.hprweb.com/2017/06/applying-six-offline-models-to-online-evangelization/.

Servais, Jacques. "Intervista al Papa emerito Benedetto." L'Osservatore Romano, March 17, 2016.

Smith, Christian, and Melinda Lundquist Denton. *Soul Searching: The Religious and Spiritual Lives of American Teenagers.* New York: Oxford University Press, 2005.

Smith, Christian, and Patricia Snell. *Souls in Transition: The Religious and Spiritual Lives of Emerging Adults.* New York: Oxford University Press, 2009.

Smith, Christian, et al. *Young Catholic America: Emerging Adults in, out of, and Gone from the Church.* New York: Oxford University Press, 2014.

Snijders, Jan. "Evangelii Nuntiandi: The Movements of Minds." *Clergy Review* 62 (1977) 170–75.

Snyder, Thomas D., ed. *120 Years of American Education: A Statistical Portrait.* Washington, DC: National Center for Education Statistics, 1993.

Sproul, R. C. *Defending Your Faith: An Introduction to Apologetics.* Wheaton, IL: Crossway, 2003.

Stark, Rodney, and Roger Finke. *The Churching of America, 1776–2005.* New Brunswick: Rutgers University Press, 2005.

Stetzer, Ed, et al. *Lost and Found: The Younger Unchurched and the Churches That Reach Them*. Nashville: B&H, 2009.

Stott, John. *The Contemporary Christian: Applying God's Word to Today's World*. Downers Grove: InterVarsity, 1992.

Synod of Bishops. *Instrumentum Laboris*. Vatican.va.

Taylor, Charles. *A Secular Age*. Cambridge: Harvard University Press, 2007.

Teasdale, Mark. "Review of *Conversational Evangelism* by Norman and David Geisler." *Journal of Christian Ministry* 3 (2011).

Third Council of Baltimore. *Baltimore Catechism*. 4 vols. Charlotte, NC: TAN, 1985.

Tillich, Paul. *Dynamics of Faith*. New York: Harper & Row, 1957.

Tremblay, Francois. "Geisler's Evangelistic Questions for Atheists." *The Prime Direction* (blog), March 7, 2014. https://francoistremblay.wordpress.com/2014/03/07/geislers-evangelistic-questions-for-atheists/.

Triska, Joel, and Rachel Triska. "Evangelizing Religious Nones." *Enrichment Journal* (Fall 2014) 74–81. http://enrichmentjournal.ag.org/201404/201404_074_Evangelizing_Nones.cfm.

Twenge, Jean. *Generation Me: Why Today's Young Americans Are More Confident, Assertive, Entitled—and More Miserable Than Ever Before*. New York: Atria, 2014.

———. *iGen: Why Today's Super-Connected Kids Are Growing Up Less Rebellious, More Tolerant, Less Happy—and Completely Unprepared for Adulthood—and What That Means for the Rest of Us*. New York: Atria, 2017.

United States Conference of Catholic Bishops. "Catechesis." USCCB.org. http://www.usccb.org/beliefs-and-teachings/how-we-teach/catechesis/.

———. *Rite of Christian Initiation of Adults*. Chicago: Liturgy Training, 1988.

———. *Sharing the Light of Faith: National Catechetical Directory for the US*. Washington, DC: USCCB, 1979.

———. *Sons and Daughters of the Light*. Washington, DC: USCCB, 1996.

———. "Young Adult Ministry." USCCB.org. https://www.usccb.org/topics/youth-and-young-adult-ministries/young-adult-ministry.

Urbano, Ryan. "Approaching the Divine: Levinas on God, Religion, Idolatry, and Atheism." *Logos: A Journal of Catholic Thought and Culture* 15 (Winter 2012) 50–81.

Van Dop, Stephen W. "Connecting to God: Exploring the Language, Motivation, and Three Strategic Evidences in Conversion to Christ." DMin diss., Asbury Theological Seminary, 2004.

Vatican Council II. "Ad Gentes." In *Vatican II: The Conciliar and Post Conciliar Documents*, edited by Austin Flannery. Collegeville, MN: Liturgical, 1980.

———. "Apostolicam Actuositatem." In *Vatican II: The Conciliar and Post Conciliar Documents*, edited by Austin Flannery. Collegeville, MN: Liturgical, 1980.

———. "Gaudium et Spes." In *Vatican II: The Conciliar and Post Conciliar Documents*, edited by Austin Flannery. Collegeville, MN: Liturgical, 1980.

———. "Lumen Gentium." In *Vatican II: The Conciliar and Post Conciliar Documents*, edited by Austin Flannery. Collegeville, MN: Liturgical, 1980.

———. "Unitatis Redintegratio." In *Vatican II: The Conciliar and Post Conciliar Documents*, edited by Austin Flannery. Collegeville, MN: Liturgical, 1980.

Vidmar, John. *The Catholic Church Through the Ages: A History*. Mahwah, NJ: Paulist, 2000.

Vielma, Sarah Anne. "The Catholic Conversion Process Among University Students: An Exploratory Study." Bachelor honors thesis, Texas State University, 2013.

Vogt, Brandon. *The Church and New Media: Blogging Converts, Online Activists, and Bishops Who Tweet.* Huntington, IN: Our Sunday Visitor, 2011.

Weddell, Sheri. *Forming Intentional Disciples: The Path to Knowing and Following Jesus.* Huntington, IN: Our Sunday Visitor, 2012.

Wellum, Stephen J. "Francis A. Schaeffer (1912–1984): Lessons from His Thought and Life." *Southern Baptist Journal of Theology* 6 (Summer 2002) 4–32.

White, James Emery. *Meet Generation Z: Understanding and Reaching the New Post-Christian World.* Grand Rapids: Baker, 2017.

———. *Rethinking the Church: A Challenge to Creative Redesign in an Age of Transition.* Grand Rapids: Baker, 2003.

———. *The Rise of the Nones: Understanding and Reaching the Religiously Unaffiliated.* Grand Rapids: Baker, 2014.

Wodehouse, Helen. "Martin Buber's I and Thou." *Philosophy* 20 (April 1945) 17–30.

Wuthnow, Robert. *After the Baby Boomers: How Twenty and Thirty-Somethings Are Changing the Church.* Princeton: Princeton University Press, 2007.

———. *The God Problem: Expressing Faith and Being Reasonable.* Berkeley: University of California Press, 2012.

———. *Loose Connections: Joining Together in America's Fragmented Communities.* Cambridge: Harvard University Press, 1998.

"Young Souls in Transition: An Interview with Christian Smith." *Yale University Reflections,* 2014. http://reflections.yale.edu/article/seeking-light-new-generation/young-souls -transition-interview-christian-smith.